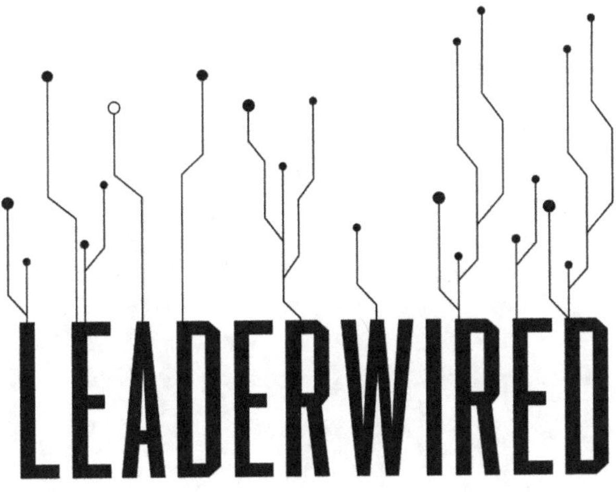
LEADERWIRED

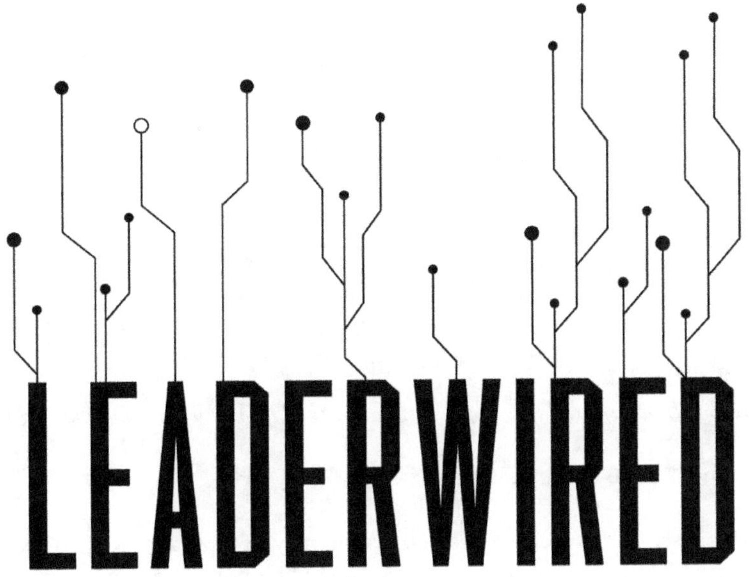

LEADERWIRED

THE AI-ERA LEADERSHIP PLAYBOOK
FOR TRANSFORMING HOW YOU
THINK, DECIDE AND LEAD

ANNA BARNHILL, MCC

LEADERWIRED
The AI-Era Leadership Playbook for Transforming How You Think, Decide and Lead

Copyright © 2026 by Anna Barnhill

Published by Alpha Abundance Press LLC
Medford, Oregon
www.Leaderwired.com

ISBN 979-8-9946493-1-2 (paperback)
ISBN *979-8-9946493-2-9* (hardcover)
ISBN *979-8-9946493-3-6* (eBook)

First Edition

"You don't need a new strategy. You need a new operating system."
— *Anna Barnhill*

Leaderwired reframes leadership transformation by focusing not on new behaviors, but on the internal operating systems that shape how leaders think, decide, behave and act. Drawing on academic rigor, neuroscience-informed insight, and deep experience developing senior leaders, Anna Barnhill offers a clear framework for why so many transformation efforts fall short in the AI era. Her book challenges the reader with insightful questions and self-examination of our thinking systems. As someone who has long championed leadership development and its relationship to technology transformation, I see this book as a timely and substantive contribution to how we prepare leaders for the future of work.

— *Jill Bruning, Chief Technology Officer, Amentum*

TABLE OF CONTENTS

FOREWORD

We all have some familiarity with change and most often observe it as happening around us - yes, impacting the environment in which we live and work - but seen as largely personal and discretionary as to how and if we adopt and adapt. Some of the most fundamental changes in our lifetimes - like the move from analogue to digital or wired to wireless - afforded choice as to whether and how to respond and react, how to operate, how to lead.

Enter the world of AI - a true paradigm shift - a level of fundamental change that demands a response from each and every one of us, but for which our traditional and incrementalist approach to change is simply obsolete, defunct. Take that reality to the organization and one quickly realizes that if the pace of change inside is incapable of matching the pace of change outside, then you are hurtling toward obsolescence and leaders have no choice but to reset, rewire to adapt, to embrace.

Having had the privilege as a CEO to lead during periods of change and transformation in very large corporate organizations such as Verizon Wireless over 25 years, I have learned that the one essential ingredient to effective leadership is an understanding that leadership must happen at every level of an organization. Throughout that journey, I have focused on ensuring authenticity by applying a very personal style to the structure and process of management - taking the role of Chief Cheerleader and Chief Storyteller, using my natural narrative style to align the organization around a common context, easily understood and readily actionable from the boardroom through to the colleagues directly engaging with your customers every day. This context, underpinned by a compelling and consistent narrative, is the secret weapon that activates effective change and transformation and allows everyone to participate in success.

Where change often fails is the assumption that it is driven exclusively top down, but an aligned context gives people at every level the confidence to exercise their judgment in how their role enables effective change. It was that conviction that first drew me to Anna Barnhill's work. Having worked with her and her students in the past, I was struck by her ability to articulate what so many leaders feel but rarely say out loud: the way we've always led isn't working anymore. It's not that we've forgotten how to lead - it's that the world has changed faster than we have. The strategies, mindsets, and behaviors that once propelled us forward now hold us back.

That's why Leaderwired is such a timely and necessary book. It's not just another leadership manual filled with tips and tricks. It's a call to action - a blueprint for rewiring the very foundation of how we think, decide, and lead in an era defined by complexity and transformation. Anna doesn't ask us to abandon who we are as leaders. Instead, she invites us to become more fully ourselves by upgrading the operating systems that shape our leadership.

This book is a companion to a complex and challenging leadership journey and Anna is the sherpa you want by your side. She doesn't shy away from the hard truths about why we get stuck, nor does she sugarcoat the discomfort of change. But she also brings a deep sense of empathy and wisdom, born from her own experiences and thousands of hours coaching leaders through their own transformations. Her stories are not just compelling; they're mirrors. You'll see yourself in their struggles, their breakthroughs, and their growth.

What makes Leaderwired stand out is its architecture. In my experience, most leadership books offer a single insight stretched across too many pages. Anna has built something fundamentally different - a comprehensive, multi-layered system that moves from personal transformation to team culture to the unique challenge of leading through AI. Each layer builds on the last. The result is not a collection of disconnected ideas but a complete operating system for leadership in an era that demands one - an era where leadership EQ may well be valued above IQ, which AI will deliver in abundance.

What I love most about Leaderwired is its honesty. Anna doesn't pretend this work is easy. She acknowledges the discomfort, the setbacks, and the slow progress that come with rewiring patterns that have been running for decades. But she also shows us what's possible when we commit to the journey. Leaders who do this work don't just become more effective - they become more aligned, more human, and more fulfilled.

As you turn these pages, you'll find yourself nodding in recognition, pausing to reflect, and maybe even feeling a little uncomfortable. That's a good thing. Discomfort is where growth begins. The world is changing faster than ever, AI is accelerating everything, and complexity is the new normal. But as Anna reminds us, the future belongs to leaders who are willing to upgrade. So let Anna help you take ownership of the next exciting chapter of your leadership journey.

Let's begin.

Ronan Dunne

Former CEO, Verizon Wireless

PART ONE

DIAGNOSIS

Recognizing the Upgrade You Need

THE OPERATING SYSTEM CRISIS

Why the Leaders Who Succeeded Before Are Failing Now

The silence in the boardroom lasted exactly four seconds. It felt like an hour.

Jackie had just said the words she couldn't take back: "We don't have the luxury of moving at the pace of the most resistant person in the room."

She watched Dr. Martinez, her Chief Medical Officer, the man who had championed her appointment to COO three years ago, look down at his notes. The other executives studied their laptops. Nobody met her eyes.

In that silence, Jackie saw herself through their eyes: not the visionary leader driving digital transformation, but the anxious executive who had lost connection with her own values. She sounded exactly like the command-and-control leaders she'd spent her career criticizing.

The ones who confused urgency with importance. The ones who left trails of burned-out direct reports and abandoned principles.

The ones she'd promised herself, standing in her first leadership role fifteen years ago, she would never become.

Four hours later, she found herself standing in a hospital corridor, fluorescent lights buzzing overhead, staring at a text from her husband: *Kids are asleep. You okay?* She couldn't remember the last time she'd tucked them in.

The irony wasn't lost on her. She'd spent eighteen months leading a patient experience transformation - preaching about human connection, about care, about what really matters in healthcare - while systematically eliminating human connection from her own life. Eighty-hour weeks. Missed recitals. Her daughter had stopped asking if she'd be at soccer games. Her son had started calling her assistant to find out if she'd make it home for dinner.

Her track record spoke for itself: regulatory compliance rates that set industry benchmarks, operational costs reduced by hundreds of millions over the past decade, a team that had followed her through two different organizations because they trusted her leadership. She had earned every promotion. Her expertise was genuine. Her commitment was unquestionable.

And yet.

The transformation was stalling. Not from lack of investment, the board had approved everything she'd requested. Not from lack of strategy, the roadmap was sound. It was stalling because of *her*. Her instincts kept conflicting with what she knew needed to happen.

She understood, intellectually, that transforming patient experience required experimentation, tolerance for ambiguity, and empowering frontline teams to make decisions without waiting for executive approval. She'd read the research. She could give a compelling presentation on adaptive leadership and the failures of command-and-control in complex environments. She had given that presentation, multiple times, to standing ovations.

But when a pilot program in the oncology unit showed mixed early results, her instinct was to step in and fix it rather than let the team learn through iteration. When department managers came to her with problems, she provided solutions instead of asking questions. When timelines slipped, she tightened controls rather than examining whether the controls themselves were the problem.

The harder she worked, the less effective she became. The more she tried to drive change, the more resistance she encountered, including, she was beginning to realize, from herself.

Standing in that corridor, Jackie finally named what she'd been avoiding for months: *The leadership approach that built my career is destroying it.*

She wasn't failing because she lacked capability or commitment. She was failing because she was trying to run a fundamentally new kind of challenge on the same internal operating system that had powered her previous successes. And that operating system, no matter how hard she pushed it, couldn't produce what this moment required.

Jackie isn't alone.

The Silent Crisis

Across industries and around the world, a silent crisis is unfolding. The most capable leaders - the ones who built impressive track records, who have genuine expertise, who care deeply about getting things right - are experiencing a strange new kind of failure.

They're not failing because they're incompetent. They're failing because the world has changed faster than their internal systems can process.

Consider the math that should keep every executive awake at night:

Seventy percent of transformation initiatives fail to achieve their stated goals. Not because the strategies are wrong, but because the leaders implementing them are running new demands on outdated internal operating systems. The knowing-doing gap that has always plagued organizations has become a chasm. Leaders know what needs to happen. They just can't make themselves do it consistently.

The half-life of leadership skills is shrinking dramatically. What worked three years ago may already be insufficient. The certainty and control that defined great leadership in 2015 are liabilities in 2025. Skills that took years to develop can become obsolete in months.

AI is reshaping leadership faster than leaders are reshaping themselves. While organizations race to implement AI in operations, customer service, and decision-making, the humans leading those implementations are often the biggest bottleneck; not because they resist AI, but because their operating systems can't process the complexity AI creates. They're trying to lead exponential change with linear internal architectures.

The conventional explanation is that "change is hard" and "people resist the unfamiliar." But that misses what's actually happening. These aren't resistant people. They're smart, committed, capable leaders whose internal systems simply weren't built for the demands they now face.

They're not broken. Their operating systems are outdated.

The Screensaver Moment

A few weeks ago, I had a conversation with my husband that perfectly captures what I mean by an outdated operating system.

He noticed I'd left my laptop open for hours without a screensaver running. "You really should use a screensaver," he said. "You're going to destroy your monitor."

I looked up from what I was doing. "Why do I need a screensaver?"

"To save the screen," he replied, as if this were obvious.

"But *why* does the screen need saving?"

I watched something shift in his expression. His words started to slow down. "Because if you leave an image on the screen too long, it..." He paused. "It burns into the..." Another pause, his pace slowing even further as the realization dawned. "Actually, I don't think I know."

He pulled out his phone and asked AI for the answer. What came back was a lightbulb moment: screensavers became essentially obsolete around 2010. Modern LCD and LED screens don't suffer from the burn-in that plagued old CRT monitors. The problem screensavers solved hasn't existed for over a decade.

My husband had been running "screensaver protocol" for fifteen years after it stopped being useful - not because he was unintelligent, but because the belief had been installed when it was true and had never been examined since.

After the laughter subsided, I asked him: "I wonder where else this shows up in our lives? Where we believe something that was true in the past without ever examining if those beliefs are still true and serving current reality?"

He got quiet. So did I.

Because the answer, of course, is *everywhere*.

This is the essence of an outdated operating system. It's not dramatic or obvious. It's thousands of small beliefs, assumptions, and patterns that were installed when they were useful and have been running ever since - never questioned, never updated, invisible in their operation but powerful in their effects.

Your leadership operating system is full of screensavers - beliefs and behaviors that made perfect sense when they were installed but are now creating friction without your awareness. The certainty that served you as an early-career expert. The control that protected you when you had less organizational power. The self-sufficiency that helped you prove yourself in competitive environments. All of these may be running long past their expiration date.

The question isn't whether you have outdated patterns. You do. We all do.

The question is whether you're willing to examine them.

The Operating System You Didn't Know You Had

Every computer runs on an operating system - the foundational software that determines how the machine processes information, manages resources, and executes commands. When you install a new application, it runs on top of this operating system. If the OS is outdated, even the most sophisticated software will lag, crash, or fail to function at all. No amount of new applications can compensate for a fundamental mismatch between what you're asking the system to do and what it was designed to handle.

Leaders have operating systems too.

Your leadership OS is the underlying architecture of thoughts, beliefs, mental models, emotional patterns, behavioral defaults, values, and communication habits that determine how you process reality and respond to it. It's the invisible layer beneath your skills and knowledge - the system that shapes how you actually show up when the pressure is on, when the stakes are high, when there's no playbook to follow.

This operating system wasn't installed at random. It was built over years, even decades, through education, early career experiences, organizational cultures, successes and failures, mentors and role models, rewards and punishments. Every leadership lesson you absorbed, every feedback session that shaped your approach, every crisis that taught you what works - all of it contributed code to your internal OS.

Most of this code was written without your conscious awareness. You didn't sit down and decide, "I will believe that leaders must have all the answers." That belief was installed through watching how authority figures were treated when they admitted uncertainty. You didn't choose to suppress emotion under pressure—you learned it by observing what happened to people who showed vulnerability in your early career environments.

For most of your career, this operating system served you well. The patterns you developed helped you navigate complexity, build credibility, and deliver results. Your decisiveness, your expertise, your ability to maintain control under pressure—these weren't accidents. They were features of an operating system optimized for a particular environment.

The problem is that the environment has fundamentally changed.

And your operating system hasn't kept pace.

You're running 2025 challenges on a 2015 operating system; or in some cases - on an operating system that was architected in 1995, when the world was unrecognizably different.

When Strengths Become Liabilities

Here's the most counterintuitive truth about leadership in this moment: *the safest strategy is now the riskiest one.*

For decades, good leaders protected their organizations from failure. The safest path was proven approaches and incremental change. Prudent management meant avoiding unnecessary risk. But transformation requires experimentation with uncertain outcomes. Organizations that won't experiment won't learn fast enough to compete, or to survive. Playing it safe has become the riskiest strategy of all.

This inversion isn't isolated. It's happening across every capability that built successful careers over the past two decades.

The Certainty Trap. A manufacturing executive I worked with had built his reputation on decisiveness. "My team knows that when I make a call, it's final," he told me proudly in our first session. Six months later, his company had missed two major market shifts because his team had stopped bringing him information that contradicted his decisions. His certainty, the very quality that had earned him the corner office, had become a liability that was blinding the organization.

Leaders were valued for having answers, for cutting through ambiguity with confident direction. But today's complex challenges often defy pattern-matching from past experience. AI surfaces possibilities that defy intuition. The pace of change means that by the time you're certain, the opportunity has passed. The new currency isn't having answers—it's asking better questions.

The Control Paradox. Effective leaders once stayed close to details, reviewed important decisions, ensured quality through involvement. But organizations now move too fast for centralized control. While you're reviewing, competitors move. AI-enabled organizations operate at speeds that human oversight can't match. The leader who needs to review everything becomes the bottleneck that slows everything. Control, pursued directly, destroys itself.

The Expertise Paradox. Career progression meant becoming the expert. Mastery took years but delivered lasting authority. But expertise has a shorter half-life than ever. AI can master technical domains in ways humans can't compete with. The leaders who win aren't those who know the most, they're those who learn the fastest and help their teams learn alongside them. Knowledge that took years to accumulate can be obsolete in months.

This isn't a failure of leadership, it's an evolution of context. What worked brilliantly in one era becomes insufficient in the next. The capabilities that earned you your current role may be precisely what's holding your organization back.

Like screensavers, these patterns were useful once. Like screensavers, they're running long past their expiration date. Like screensavers, they're so familiar you've probably never thought to question them.

The AI Acceleration

Every shift described above is now accelerating because of AI.

AI doesn't just add one more change to manage. It fundamentally alters the speed and complexity of everything else. It's not a new application running on the same operating system, it's a force that exposes every limitation in your current OS and demands capabilities that many leaders have never developed.

Compressing decision timelines. AI generates insights and options faster than traditional processes can evaluate them. By the time you've processed the implications of one AI-generated recommendation, three more have arrived. The cognitive load is overwhelming, unless your operating system is built for it.

Expanding complexity exponentially. AI doesn't simplify - it reveals complexity that was always there but couldn't be processed. Leaders face more variables, more interconnections, more second-order effects than ever before. The illusion that you could understand everything has shattered.

Reshaping what "expertise" means. When AI can master technical domains overnight, human expertise shifts from *knowing* to *judging*, from having answers to asking better questions. The value you provide is no longer what you know but how you think.

Creating human-AI collaboration demands. The leaders who thrive won't be those who use AI as a tool or resist it as a threat. They'll be those who design new kinds of human-AI collaboration that neither humans nor AI could accomplish alone.

Accelerating the obsolescence of outdated operating systems. The gap between leaders running current OS and those running outdated versions is widening faster than ever. In the pre-AI era, you could coast on an outdated operating system for years before consequences became visible. Now, the gap becomes obvious in months.

This is why "waiting to see how AI plays out" is not a strategy. By the time the picture becomes clear, leaders with outdated operating systems will be too far behind to catch up. The time to upgrade is now.

The Gap Between Knowing and Doing

If you've been leading for any length of time, you've probably encountered this frustrating reality: understanding what to do differently is far easier than actually doing it.

You know you should delegate more, but when the stakes are high, you find yourself jumping in. You understand the value of psychological safety, but when someone challenges your idea in a meeting, your defenses rise before you can catch them. You've read about growth mindset, but when you face a significant setback, the old voice of self-criticism returns with full force.

This knowing-doing gap represents the greatest untapped opportunity in leadership development. And it persists because most development efforts focus on adding knowledge and skills while ignoring the mechanism that determines whether those additions can actually translate into action.

That mechanism is your operating system.

When Jackie found herself snapping at her CMO about AI time-lines, she wasn't lacking knowledge about collaborative leadership. She wasn't missing skills in facilitation or emotional intelligence. She had all of that. She was running new demands on an outdated operating system, and the old system won.

Here's what's actually happening when the gap appears:

Your conscious intentions run on the new software. You've learned new approaches, adopted new frameworks, committed to new behaviors. The updated version of yourself lives in your conscious mind, ready to be deployed.

But your automatic responses still run on the old operating system. When pressure rises, when stakes increase, when your nervous system detects threat—the old patterns take over. Not because you're weak or undisciplined. Because that's how operating systems work. They're designed to run automatically, beneath conscious awareness, especially when cognitive load is high.

The path forward isn't more knowledge. It isn't trying harder. It isn't another conference or another book added to the pile of things you know but don't do.

The path forward is upgrading the operating system itself.

The Integration Imperative

Through years of working with leaders across industries, I've identified a pattern in how sustainable leadership transformation actually happens, and why it so often doesn't.

Most leaders understand the basic cycle of achievement: ambition leads to planning, planning leads to knowledge, knowledge leads to action. This cycle makes logical sense. It's how we've been taught to approach professional development since the earliest stages of our careers.

And yet, for many leaders, it produces disappointing results. They cycle through ambition, planning, knowledge and action - and find themselves back where they started, frustrated that nothing has fundamentally changed.

What's missing? The element that sits at the center of the cycle and determines whether everything else actually works: **integration**.

Integration is the process of harmonizing your ambition, planning, knowledge, and action so that your efforts become purposeful, coherent, and aligned with your vision and values. It's the linchpin that transforms intellectual understanding into embodied capability - that turns what you know into who you are.

This is precisely what Jackie experienced. She had the ambition, no one could question her commitment to transformation. She had the planning—her strategy was sound. She had the knowledge, she could articulate what needed to happen. And she had action, she was working eighty-hour weeks. But she hadn't done the integration work. Her inner game remained unchanged. So, every new insight she gained ran into the same outdated operating system, producing the same frustrating results.

Here's the connection that changes everything: **integration is what a properly functioning leadership operating system produces.**

When your OS is upgraded - when your beliefs, mindsets, emotional processing, thought patterns, behavioral defaults, values alignment, and communication protocols are all working together coherently - integration happens naturally. Your ambition aligns with your actions. Your knowledge translates into capability. The gap between knowing and doing begins to close, not through willpower, but through architecture.

The Cost of Running Outdated Software

The consequences of operating system mismatch extend far beyond individual frustration. They ripple through teams, cultures, and entire organizations.

Friction and burnout. When your internal OS can't process the demands being placed on it, everything takes more effort than it should. You find yourself working harder with diminishing returns. The exhaustion isn't just physical, it's the deep fatigue of constantly fighting your own patterns.

Cascading cultural effects. Leaders running outdated operating systems create environments that reflect those limitations. Teams develop avoidance patterns, resistance behaviors, and protective adaptations. Talent leaves for environments where they can do their best work.

Failed AI integration. Organizations invest millions in AI technology that threatens their people or challenges their leaders' mental models. Leaders running threat-response OS communicate anxiety about AI that spreads through their organizations. The technology works; the leadership doesn't.

The cumulative cost is staggering - not just in dollars, though research suggests that ineffective leadership costs organizations billions annually. The deeper cost is in human potential left unrealized:

the innovations that weren't built, the transformations that weren't led, the futures that didn't happen because the leadership capacity wasn't there.

Why This Book, Why Me

I didn't learn about outdated operating systems from a textbook. I learned by running one, and nearly crashing because of it.

I grew up in Soviet Ukraine during the final decades of communism, in a culture with rigid rules about who you could be and how you were allowed to show up. Emotions were considered weakness. Conformity was survival. As a female who was also left-handed, unusually intelligent and eventually came out as bisexual in a violently intolerant environment, I learned early that the parts of myself that didn't fit the system had to be hidden or suppressed.

In that world, I developed an operating system optimized for constraint. I learned to read subtle cues, navigate complex group dynamics, suppress what didn't fit, and perform whatever version of myself the system required. These weren't conscious choices, they were adaptations encoded into my internal architecture through years of necessity.

When I eventually built a career in the West - earning advanced degrees, climbing to executive roles, becoming one of the youngest members of a publicly traded company's leadership team, I assumed I had left that old operating system behind. I was successful, after all. The evidence suggested the system was working.

Then, in 2013, my body delivered a message I couldn't ignore. A cancer scare, caught early but jarring enough to crack the illusion of invincibility. Then bilateral knee surgeries that forced me to stop moving for a year.

In that stillness, I finally heard what my spirit had been whispering for decades: *the operating system I was running wasn't mine.* It had been installed by a culture I no longer lived in, optimized for survival in conditions that no longer applied. And it was slowly destroying me.

That year became my catalyst. I examined beliefs I didn't know I held. I questioned patterns I had assumed were just "who I am." Slowly, painfully, and then with increasing clarity, I upgraded.

What I discovered in that process became the foundation for everything I now teach. Over the past 16 years, I've refined these frameworks through thousands of hours of executive coaching, through teaching leadership and innovation at MIT Professional Education, through writing for Forbes, through working with leaders at startups and Fortune 500 companies across healthcare, technology, financial services and aerospace.

I've seen what works. I've seen what doesn't. And I've learned that what separates leaders who transform from those who stay stuck isn't talent or intelligence or commitment. It's whether they do the operating system work.

I wrote this book because I believe this work shouldn't require a crisis to initiate. And I wrote it because this moment - with AI reshaping every industry, with complexity accelerating beyond any individual's ability to control it - requires leaders who've done the deeper work.

The human upgrade isn't optional anymore.

What This Book Is - And What It Isn't

This is not a book of tips and tricks. It's not a collection of frameworks you'll understand intellectually and then struggle to apply. It's not another set of best practices that assumes your internal system is ready to execute them.

This is a playbook for rewiring the architecture that prevents you from being what you already know you should be.

It's built on what I call the 7-5-3 Human Upgrade Code™:

Seven operating system components - beliefs, mindsets, emotional processing, thought patterns, behavioral defaults, values alignment, and communication protocols - form the internal architecture that gets upgraded.

Five premium skillsets - cognitive flexibility, emotional intelligence at scale, human-AI collaboration design, strategic sensemaking, and exponential thinking - emerge when those upgraded components work together in integration.

Three system foundations - Curiosity, Care, and Courage - create cultural infrastructure that enables individual upgrades to scale through teams and organizations.

The **Five AI Leadership Shifts™** - covered in Chapter Thirteen - show you how to apply this timeless architecture to the current moment of AI transformation.

The Journey Ahead

The book is organized in four parts:

Part One: Diagnosis (Chapters 1-3) establishes the foundation. You'll learn the anatomy of an outdated operating system, see how your current patterns developed, and understand why the upgrade imperative is so urgent in the AI era.

Part Two: Internal Architecture (Chapters 4-10) takes you deep into the seven components of your leadership operating system - beliefs, mindsets, emotional processing, thought patterns, behavioral defaults, values, and communication protocols. Each chapter shows you what an upgrade looks like and how to implement it.

Part Three: From Insight to Integration (Chapter 11) reveals what emerges when upgraded components work together - the five premium skillsets that define AI-era leadership: cognitive flexibility, emotional intelligence at scale, human-AI collaboration design, strategic sensemaking, and exponential thinking.

Part Four: Scaling at Systems Level (Chapters 12-14) shows how to extend your personal transformation into collective capacity. The House of Empathy™ framework creates conditions where others can upgrade too, you'll learn specifically how to lead AI transformation in ways that most leaders get wrong, and you'll establish practices for ongoing development.

An Invitation

I won't pretend this work is easy. Upgrading your operating system means examining patterns you've relied on for years, possibly decades. It means sitting with discomfort rather than rushing to resolve it. It means accepting that some of what made you successful will not make you successful going forward, especially as AI reshapes what leadership requires.

But I will tell you this: the leaders who do this work report something unexpected. They describe not just greater effectiveness, but greater ease. Not working harder, but working differently, in a way that feels more aligned with who they actually are. The friction that consumed so much energy begins to dissolve. The gap between knowing and doing starts to close. And the capabilities the AI era demands - cognitive flexibility, emotional intelligence at scale, strategic sensemaking amid complexity - begin to emerge naturally from the upgraded foundation.

Jackie, the healthcare executive standing in that hospital corridor at night, eventually made the shift. It required her to do something that didn't come naturally: stop trying to fix the transformation and start examining the operating system she was bringing to it.

Through focused work on her leadership OS, upgrading her beliefs about what leadership required, rewiring her emotional processing patterns, building new behavioral defaults, Jackie found what she came to call her "strong ground." A foundation of clarity about who she was as a leader that didn't depend on having all the answers or maintaining control of every variable.

The results showed up in ways both measurable and intangible. Patient experience scores began moving. Middle managers who had been resisting started engaging. Teams that had felt overwhelmed found their footing. Jackie started getting home for dinner.

But something else emerged that Jackie hadn't anticipated. As her organization began integrating AI into clinical workflows, she noticed she was leading differently than her peers at other health systems. Where others resisted or over-relied on the technology, Jackie approached it with curiosity. Where others struggled to help their teams adapt, Jackie created psychological safety for experimentation. The upgraded operating system hadn't just made her more effective - it had made her AI-ready.

"I used to feel like I was translating all the time," she told me months later. "Like the leader I needed to be was somehow different from who I actually was. Now I understand - I wasn't lacking anything. I just needed to upgrade the system that was processing everything. Once I found my strong ground, everything else started to flow, including how I lead through all this change."

That's the journey this book offers. Not becoming someone different but becoming more fully who you already are, with an operating system capable of expressing it. An operating system built for this moment.

The future belongs to leaders who make this upgrade. The question isn't whether you're capable of it. You are.

The question is whether you're ready to begin.

THE ANATOMY OF AN OUTDATED OPERATING SYSTEM

Understanding What's Running Beneath Your Awareness

"If I don't do it, who will?"

I asked Marcus to sit with that phrase. He'd just said it to me in our first coaching session, explaining why he had to be involved in every significant decision at his firm. It seemed so reasonable when he said it - a statement of responsibility, of commitment, of leadership.

"How long have you been operating from that belief?" I asked.

He paused. Something shifted in his expression, a door opening to a room he hadn't visited in a long time.

"Since I was twelve," he said quietly. "When my dad got sick. I was the oldest of four kids. Mom was working two jobs and trying to take care of him. If I didn't handle things at home, nobody would."

That's the moment Marcus discovered his operating system.

A belief installed three decades earlier, in response to a family crisis, was still running his leadership. It had been useful then, essential even. A twelve-year-old stepping up when his family needed him. But it had never been examined, never updated, never questioned. And now it was destroying the very organization it had once helped him save.

Marcus had built his reputation on being the one who could handle anything. During the financial crisis of 2008, when his firm was hemorrhaging clients and partners were jumping ship, he was the one everyone turned to. He worked eighteen-hour days, personally managing relationships that others had written off, making decisions that needed making when everyone else was paralyzed by uncertainty. The firm survived, barely, and his reputation was sealed. Marcus was the guy who could save you when things got desperate.

A decade later, his firm was thriving again, but Marcus wasn't. The same leadership approach that had saved the company was now suffocating it. His direct reports had stopped bringing him problems because he always had solutions - which meant they never developed the capability to solve things themselves. Innovation had stalled because every new idea had to survive his scrutiny before it could move forward. The best people were leaving, citing "lack of growth opportunity" - code for "Marcus won't let go."

The turning point came during a 360-degree feedback process that his board had mandated. The results weren't just disappointing, they were devastating. Words like "micromanager" and "bottleneck" appeared repeatedly. One observation cut deepest: "Marcus doesn't trust anyone to do anything important without him."

Like a screensaver protecting monitors that no longer exist, his pattern was solving a problem that was no longer his to solve.

Your Version of This Story

Before we go further, pause for a moment.

What's *your* version of "if I don't do it, who will"? Every leader has one - a phrase, a belief, a pattern that feels like bedrock truth but is actually ancient code still running.

Maybe yours is "I have to prove myself constantly." Maybe it's "People will let you down if you give them the chance." Maybe it's "Showing uncertainty is showing weakness." Maybe it's "I need to work twice as hard as everyone else to be taken seriously."

Whatever it is, it probably served you once. It probably still feels true. And it's probably creating friction you've been attributing to external circumstances.

Hold that phrase in mind as you read this chapter. We're going to examine how these patterns get built, and why they persist long after they've stopped serving you.

How Operating Systems Get Built

You weren't born with your leadership operating system. It was constructed, layer by layer, through decades of experience, adaptation, and unconscious encoding. Understanding how it got built is the first step toward upgrading it.

The Foundation Layer: Early Programming

The deepest layers of your operating system were installed before you had language to describe them. Your family system taught you fundamental beliefs about authority, conflict, achievement, and emotional expression. Were mistakes punished or treated as learning opportunities? Was vulnerability safe or dangerous? Did love feel conditional on performance?

These early experiences didn't just shape your childhood, they created the foundational code that still runs beneath your conscious awareness decades later.

Consider how powerful this early programming is. A child who learned that expressing anger resulted in withdrawal of love learns to suppress anger. Thirty years later, that child, now an executive, struggles to give direct feedback because anger still feels dangerous. The conscious mind knows feedback is necessary. The operating system still runs the old code: *Anger equals danger. Suppress to survive.*

Cultural context added another layer. The society you grew up in transmitted messages about success, failure, gender, power, and belonging. I experienced this firsthand. Growing up in Soviet Ukraine, I absorbed an operating system optimized for constraint, where emotions were weakness, conformity was survival, and being different made you a target. That system served a purpose in that context. But it also installed beliefs I carried long after I left, running silently beneath my conscious choices like background software I never agreed to install.

The Professional Layer: Career Encoding

As you entered the professional world, your operating system continued to develop. Early career experiences carried disproportionate weight - the first boss who shaped your understanding of leadership, the initial successes that taught you what worked, the early failures that installed protective patterns you still run today.

Think about your first significant professional success. What did it teach you about how to succeed? Whatever worked then got encoded: the long hours, the self-reliance, the attention to detail, the ability to produce under pressure. These patterns didn't just help you once, they became part of your operating system.

Organizations function as operating system developers. Every company has implicit rules about what gets rewarded, what gets punished, and what gets ignored. You learned to read these signals and adapt accordingly. The leader praised for decisiveness learned to value certainty. The manager rewarded for tight control learned to fear delegation. Each adaptation made sense at the time. Each pattern that got encoded helped you survive and advance.

The problem is that encoding happens automatically, beneath conscious awareness. You don't choose to install these patterns, they install themselves through reinforcement. What works gets repeated. What gets repeated becomes automatic. What becomes automatic becomes invisible.

The Success Layer: When Strengths Become Shadows

Here's the paradox that makes this work so challenging: your greatest strengths are often the most deeply encoded patterns, and therefore the hardest to see and the most resistant to change.

When Marcus discovered his "if I don't do it, who will" pattern, he wasn't uncovering a weakness. He was seeing the shadow side of one of his greatest strengths. His willingness to take responsibility, to step up when others stepped back - these qualities had been essential to his success. But strengths encoded without awareness become compulsions. The helpful pattern becomes an unconscious obligation. The thing that once served you begins to run you.

This is why high performers often struggle most with operating system upgrades. Their patterns are more deeply encoded precisely because those patterns produced exceptional results.

When Patterns Collide with Reality

Sarah had risen through the ranks of a major technology company on the strength of her analytical rigor. She was the one who could find the flaw in any proposal, the gap in any strategy, the risk that everyone else had missed. Her critical thinking had saved her organization from costly mistakes countless times.

When she was promoted to lead the company's AI integration initiative, she brought the same approach. Every vendor proposal was scrutinized for weaknesses. Every pilot program was analyzed for potential failures. Every team recommendation was questioned, challenged, refined.

Within six months, the initiative had stalled. Not because Sarah's analysis was wrong, it was impeccable. But because the same critical lens that had protected the organization from bad decisions was now preventing it from making any decisions at all.

Sarah was running an operating system optimized for risk prevention in an environment that required risk tolerance. Her greatest strength - the ability to see what could go wrong - had become her greatest limitation.

"I kept waiting until I was sure," she told me. "But with AI, you're never sure. By the time you're sure, you're behind."

Where Is This Showing Up for You?

Sarah's story illustrates a pattern you may recognize: a strength that served you brilliantly in one context becoming a liability in another.

Consider: What capability built your career? Was it your attention to detail? Your ability to see around corners? Your capacity to push through obstacles? Your talent for bringing people together?

Now ask the harder question: Where might that same capability be creating friction today? The attention to detail that becomes micro-management. The strategic foresight that becomes analysis paralysis. The drive that becomes burnout. The relationship focus that becomes conflict avoidance.

The strength itself isn't the problem. The problem is when it runs automatically, without conscious choice, in contexts where it no longer fits.

The Seven Components of Your Leadership OS

Your operating system isn't a single monolithic program. It's a complex architecture of seven interconnected components, each influencing the others, together determining how you process reality and respond to it.

I'll introduce all seven here, but three deserve deeper attention because they're where most leaders experience the most friction in the AI era.

1. Belief Architecture: The Bedrock

At the foundation sits your belief architecture - the fundamental assumptions you hold about yourself, others, and how the world works. These aren't beliefs you consciously chose. They were installed through experience and have been running so long they feel like facts rather than interpretations.

"I have to prove myself constantly." "People can't be trusted to follow through." "Conflict is dangerous." "I need to have the answers to be credible." These beliefs operate as the bedrock layer of your OS, shaping everything built on top of them.

Here's what makes belief architecture so powerful: you don't experience beliefs as beliefs. You experience them as *reality*. Marcus didn't think he *believed* he had to handle everything himself - he experienced it as simply true, as the way the world worked. That's what made it so hard to see and so resistant to change.

The AI-era challenge: If your belief architecture includes "I need to have the answers to be credible," you'll struggle profoundly with AI systems that generate answers faster than you can. Your credibility feels threatened every time someone asks Claude instead of asking you. That's not a rational response, it's your operating system protecting a belief that may have been true in 2015 but is actively harmful in 2025.

2. Mindsets: The Orientation Layer

If beliefs are the bedrock, mindsets are the orientation layer - the default settings that determine how you approach challenges, uncertainty and change.

Five mindset shifts prove particularly critical for AI-era leadership:

From certainty to curiosity - embracing not-knowing as strength rather than weakness

From control to orchestration - designing systems rather than managing outputs

From expertise to learning velocity - valuing how fast you learn over how much you know

From risk avoidance to experimentation - treating failure as data rather than disaster

From individual decisions to collaborative intelligence - building collective capacity rather than personal authority

Sarah's story is a mindset story. Her operating system was locked in certainty-seeking mode in a context that required curiosity. She couldn't shift, not because she didn't understand the need intellectually, but because her mindset ran automatically, beneath conscious choice.

3. Emotional Processing: The Hidden Driver

Your emotional processing system determines how you experience, interpret, and respond to the constant stream of emotional data that leadership generates. And here's what most leaders don't realize: emotions drive far more of your decision-making than logic does.

Neuroscience research has established that emotions aren't separate from rational thought - they're the foundation of it. The executive who believes she makes purely logical decisions is running an outdated understanding of how her own brain works. Every decision is emotionally informed. The question is whether you're aware of the emotional inputs or blind to them.

Most leaders have been taught to manage emotions - meaning suppress them - rather than to process them effectively. The result is an emotional backlog that leaks out sideways: the irritation that seems disproportionate to the trigger, the anxiety that won't resolve, the exhaustion that rest doesn't fix.

The AI-era challenge: AI creates specific emotional challenges that most leaders are unequipped to process. Threat response to AI capability. Anxiety about uncertainty and obsolescence. Grief about roles and skills that are changing. Responsibility for human impact of AI decisions. Leaders stuck in fight-or-flight can't navigate this terrain. They either resist AI (fight) or defer to it completely (flight). Neither response serves.

The Supporting Architecture

Four additional components complete your operating system:

4. Thought Patterns - the cognitive habits that shape how you process information and make meaning. What makes thought patterns dangerous is their speed and invisibility. They run in milliseconds, beneath conscious awareness. By the time you notice a thought, it's already been filtered through patterns you didn't choose. In the AI era, these patterns get amplified: confirmation bias gets worse when AI can find evidence for anything you already believe.

5. Behavioral Defaults - the automatic responses you fall back on when pressure rises and you don't have bandwidth to be deliberate. When someone brings you a problem, what's your instinctive first move? To solve it? To ask questions? To reassure? That default wasn't chosen, it was encoded. And in the AI era, where speed demands faster responses, there's less time for conscious override. Your defaults matter more than ever.

6. Values Alignment - the degree of congruence between what you say is important, what actually drives your decisions, and how you spend your time and energy. When alignment is high, leadership feels integrated. When alignment is low, leadership feels fragmented and exhausting. AI decisions affect people in profound ways, leaders need values clarity to navigate the ethical complexity AI creates.

7. Communication Protocols - the default patterns governing how you share information, receive input, navigate conflict, and build relationships. As AI handles more transactional communication, human communication must handle the adaptive, emotional, relational work that AI can't. The bar for human communication rises precisely because routine communication can be automated.

The Interconnection Problem

These seven components don't operate independently. They form an interconnected system where each element influences the others. Dysfunction in one area ripples through the entire system.

Consider how a single limiting belief cascades:

Belief: "I must have all the answers to be respected."

Mindset impact: Defaults to certainty over curiosity. Avoids situations where not-knowing would be visible.

Emotional processing: Anxiety when encountering the unknown. Shame when unable to answer a question.

Thought patterns: Filters for confirming information. Dismisses input that challenges expertise.

Behavioral defaults: Provides answers even when unsure. Avoids asking questions that reveal gaps.

Values alignment: Time invested in appearing knowledgeable rather than actually learning.

Communication: Tells rather than asks. Struggles to say "I don't know."

One outdated belief has contaminated the entire system. This is why surface-level behavior change fails - you're treating symptoms while the underlying infection spreads.

Tracing Your Own Cascade

Return to the belief you identified at the beginning of this chapter - your version of "if I don't do it, who will."

Now trace its cascade:

How does this belief affect your default mindset? Do you approach situations with more certainty or more curiosity because of it?

What emotions does it generate? When does it create anxiety, frustration, or exhaustion?

What thought patterns does it reinforce? What information do you filter for or filter out?

What behaviors does it drive when you're under pressure?

Where does it create misalignment between your stated values and your actual choices?

How does it shape how you communicate - what you say, what you don't say, how you listen?

This tracing exercise often reveals that a single belief is responsible for friction points that seemed unrelated. The exhaustion, the conflict patterns, the sense of running on a treadmill - they may all trace back to one piece of ancient code.

The Upgrade Opportunity

The good news: operating systems can be upgraded.

Unlike hardware, which requires replacement, your internal operating system can be rewired. Neuroscience has established that the brain remains plastic throughout life - capable of forming new neural pathways, strengthening useful patterns, and weakening outdated ones. The patterns that feel permanent aren't. They just feel that way because they've been running so long.

The work isn't easy. Patterns encoded over decades don't dissolve overnight. But they can be identified, examined, and systematically replaced with patterns better suited to current conditions.

Marcus did this work. It took months, not weeks. He had to learn to notice when the twelve-year-old's code was running - the anxiety that arose when he wasn't involved in a decision, the compulsion to check on things his team was handling. He had to build new patterns: asking questions instead of providing solutions, trusting process instead of requiring oversight, measuring success by his team's capability rather than his own indispensability.

The results weren't just professional. "I realized I'd been running that pattern in my marriage too," he told me later. "Taking on everything, wondering why my wife seemed disengaged, never seeing that I was crowding her out the same way I'd crowded out my team."

Sarah's upgrade looked different. She had to learn to act before certainty - to treat her analysis as one input rather than the final word. She developed what she called "good enough" protocols: decision criteria that let her move forward without perfect information. Her AI initiative launched nine months late, but it launched. And more importantly, she had a new pattern she could apply to whatever came next.

Here's what both of them discovered: the upgrade didn't require becoming someone different. It required becoming more conscious of who they already were - and more deliberate about which patterns to run in which contexts.

That's what the rest of this book provides: a systematic methodology for upgrading each component of your leadership operating system.

But first, you need to see clearly what you're working with.

A crucial principle: *awareness precedes choice.* You cannot upgrade patterns you cannot see. The diagnostic work in the next chapter isn't just preparation for change, it's the beginning of change itself.

The moment Marcus said "since I was twelve," his operating system became visible. And in that visibility, for the first time in thirty years, it became optional.

That's the opportunity ahead of you now.

❧

MAPPING YOUR CURRENT OS

A Diagnostic Framework for Identifying Where Upgrade Is Needed

"That can't be right."

David was staring at the 360-degree feedback summary I'd just handed him. He'd been a technology VP for twelve years, promoted twice, consistently rated as a high performer. He knew who he was as a leader.

Or thought he did.

"They're saying I don't listen," he said, scanning the comments. "That I've already made up my mind before meetings start. That people have stopped bringing me ideas because..." He paused on a phrase. "Because I make them feel stupid for suggesting anything I haven't already thought of."

He looked up at me. "I ask questions in every meeting. I literally have a rule, I don't speak first. How can they say I don't listen?"

This was the moment I'd seen dozens of times before. The collision between self-perception and external reality. The instant when a leader discovers that the operating system they thought they were running is not the operating system others experience.

"Tell me about the questions you ask," I said.

He thought for a moment. "I ask people what they think. I ask if anyone sees problems with my analysis. I ask if there are considerations I'm missing."

"Your analysis," I repeated. "Problems with *your* analysis. Considerations *you're* missing."

The silence lasted several seconds.

"I'm not asking what they think," he said slowly. "I'm asking them to validate what I already think. Or to find flaws in what I've already decided."

"And when they don't find flaws?"

"I assume I was right." Another pause. "But they might just be... not trying. Because they know it won't matter."

David had just mapped his operating system. Not from the inside, where he experienced himself as curious and collaborative, but from the outside, where others experienced him as a leader who had already decided and was performing consultation rather than practicing it.

The gap between those two versions wasn't a failure of character. It was a diagnostic finding. And it pointed directly to where his upgrade needed to begin.

The Diagnostic Challenge

Here's the fundamental problem with diagnosing your own operating system: you're using the system to examine the system.

David genuinely believed he was listening. His operating system filtered his experience to confirm that belief. When he asked questions and people nodded, his system interpreted that as successful consultation. It couldn't see what it was designed not to see: that the nods were compliance, not agreement; that the silence was resignation, not satisfaction.

This is why self-reflection, while valuable, has limits. No matter how honest and curious you are, you're still looking through the lens that needs examining. The patterns most deeply encoded are often the patterns most invisible to you.

Effective diagnosis requires multiple inputs: structured self-reflection, external feedback, pattern recognition across contexts, and ideally a formal assessment. This chapter provides all of these.

But first, let's start with what you can see from the inside.

Your Starting Point

Take out a blank sheet of paper. Or open a new document on your screen.

Write down the answer to this question: *What is the single biggest friction point in your leadership right now?*

Not the external challenge - the market conditions, the difficult team member, the demanding board. The internal friction. The pattern that keeps showing up regardless of circumstance. The obstacle that seems to follow you from situation to situation.

Don't overthink it. Write the first thing that comes to mind.

Now look at what you wrote. That friction point is almost certainly a symptom of an operating system issue. It's where your current OS is colliding with your current demands. And it's the doorway into the diagnostic work of this chapter.

Mapping the Seven Components

For each component, I've provided diagnostic prompts designed to surface patterns that typically run beneath conscious awareness. Don't rush through these. The value isn't in quick answers, it's in the reflection the prompts provoke.

1. Belief Architecture

The Scenario: You're in a leadership meeting and someone asks you a question you don't know the answer to. Your entire team is watching. What happens in your body? What thought fires first? What do you do?

If you feel anxiety, if your first thought is about how you'll be perceived, if you find yourself constructing a partial answer rather than saying "I don't know" - you've just surfaced a belief about what leaders must be.

Dig deeper: Complete this sentence five different ways: "To be a successful leader, I must..." Stop now - and do it before you continue... I will be here waiting for you.

Which of these are genuine requirements, and which are beliefs that could be questioned?

What do you believe about human nature - are people fundamentally trustworthy, or do they need oversight to perform? Where did that belief come from? Is there evidence that contradicts it?

AI-era probe: When you encounter AI that can do something you used to do - answer a question, draft a document, analyze data - what's your immediate emotional response? That response reveals beliefs about where your value comes from.

2. Mindsets

Consider these pairs. Which side do you default to, not in theory, but in practice when pressure is high?

Certainty vs. Curiosity: When facing a decision with incomplete information, do you wait for more data or move forward with what you have? When's the last time you genuinely changed your mind about something significant?

Control vs. Orchestration: When something important is happening, do you need to be involved in it? Can you design systems and trust them, or do you need to oversee outputs?

Expertise vs. Learning: How do you respond when someone challenges your expertise? What happens inside you? Do you view failures as threats to your identity or as data for learning?

AI-era probe: When AI suggests a different approach than yours, what's your typical response? Dismissal? Curiosity? Threat?

3. Emotional Processing

Right now, as you read this, can you name what you're feeling with specificity beyond "fine" or "stressed"? Try it. Is there anticipation? Skepticism? Hope? Resistance? Fatigue? Something else?

The precision with which you can name emotions correlates directly with your ability to manage them. Leaders who can only access "stressed" or "frustrated" are working with a limited emotional vocabulary, and a limited capacity to use their emotions to inspire and galvanize others.

Track your patterns: When you experience strong emotion at work, what do you do with it? Suppress it? Express it? Analyze it? Avoid the situations that trigger it?

How long does it typically take you to recover equilibrium after a stressful event? Hours? Days? Do some things linger for weeks?

What emotions do you tend to suppress? What emotions do you over-express? There's diagnostic gold in both patterns.

AI-era probe: What emotions arise when you think about AI's role in your organization's future? In your own future? Name them specifically.

4 & 5. Thought Patterns and Behavioral Defaults

These two components are best diagnosed together because thought patterns drive behavioral defaults.

The Stress Test: Think about the last time you were significantly stressed at work. When something went wrong, where did your mind go first - to blame, to problem-solving, to catastrophizing, to denial? That first move reveals your thought pattern.

And what behavior followed? When someone brings you a problem, what's your instinctive first move - to solve it, to ask questions, to reassure, to delegate? When stress increases, do you push harder or pull back? When you're overwhelmed, what behavior emerges that you later regret?

The Feedback Theme: What feedback have you received repeatedly throughout your career, the theme that keeps appearing regardless of context? That recurring feedback is pointing at an operating system pattern.

AI-era probe: When you hear predictions about AI's future impact, do you dismiss them, catastrophize about them, or evaluate them critically? When faced with an AI-related decision you feel unprepared for, what do you do?

6 & 7. Values Alignment and Communication Protocols

These components are best diagnosed through evidence rather than self-report.

The Calendar Test: Reflect on your calendar for the past month. Not what you intended - what actually happened. What do your actual time allocations say about your operating values? Where is there a gap between what you say matters and how you behave?

If your team described your values based purely on observing your behavior - not listening to your words - what would they say?

The Communication Audit: When did you last receive feedback that your communication had unintended impact? How do you respond when someone disagrees with you publicly? Do people tend to give you honest feedback, or tell you what they think you want to hear?

What's the gap between how you intend to come across and how others actually experience you? If you don't know, that gap is probably larger than you think.

AI-era probe: How do you communicate about AI with your team - with anxiety, dismissiveness, or genuine engagement? Do you say you value innovation while resisting AI adoption?

What Others See That You Can't

David's story at the beginning of this chapter illustrates a universal truth: your operating system produces outputs that are visible to others but often invisible to you.

The way you show up in meetings, the tone of your emails, the patterns in how you respond to pressure - others see these clearly even when you don't. They experience the output of your operating system. You experience the intention behind it. These are often very different things.

Marcus discovered this gap vividly. He saw himself as supportive and empowering. His team experienced him as micromanaging and anxious. The disconnect wasn't about bad intent - it was about an operating system running patterns he couldn't see.

"You helped me self-reflect and self-resolve many issues," he told me later. "I resonated better with the outcomes because they came out from my exploratory process, from inside me, rather than from someone telling me what to do."

The key insight: he needed external input to see what was invisible from the inside, but the change had to come from his own discovery.

Getting External Data

360-degree feedback can reveal operating system patterns that self-reflection misses. When multiple people describe similar experiences of you, especially if their descriptions surprise you, you've found an OS pattern worth examining. Pay particular attention to the gaps: where does their experience diverge most from your self-perception?

Trusted colleagues who will tell you the truth are invaluable. Not people who will be kind, people who will be honest. Ask someone who knows you well: "What patterns do you see in me that I might not see in myself?" And then listen without defending.

Pattern recognition across contexts: If similar dynamics keep appearing with different people and in different situations, the common denominator is your operating system. The problem that follows you from role to role isn't bad luck, it's a pattern you're carrying.

Common Friction Patterns

As you analyze your diagnostic results, you may recognize yourself in these common patterns. You'll also recognize the leaders we've already met.

The Certainty Trap: High expertise + fixed mindset + discomfort with uncertainty = difficulty leading in complexity. *This was Sarah's pattern* - her analytical rigor became paralysis when certainty wasn't available. Leaders in this trap keep waiting for enough information to be sure, not realizing that in the AI era, certainty arrives too late to matter.

The Control Paradox: Strong ownership + weak delegation + perfectionism = bottleneck leadership. *This was Marcus's pattern* - his "if I don't do it, who will" belief created an organization that couldn't function without him. Leaders in this trap work harder and harder while their organizations become less and less capable.

The Emotional Bypass: Emotional suppression + task focus + efficiency drive = disconnection from self and others. Leaders in this trap pride themselves on being "rational" while their unprocessed emotions leak out sideways - in irritation, exhaustion or relationships that never deepen beyond transactional.

The Expertise Anchor: Identity tied to knowing + authority from expertise + discomfort asking questions = struggle in learning environments. *This was David's pattern* - his questions weren't questions at all, just invitations to validate what he'd already decided. Leaders in this trap feel threatened by AI precisely because their identity is built on knowing things that AI can now know faster.

The Values Gap: Clear stated values + competing pressures + insufficient boundaries = chronic misalignment. *This was Jackie's pattern* - she valued human connection while systematically eliminating it from her own life. Leaders in this trap feel perpetually fragmented, working hard but never feeling aligned.

Which patterns do you recognize in yourself? Most leaders have elements of several. The question is which ones are creating the most friction in your current context.

Finding Your Friction Points

Having examined each component, step back and look at the system as a whole. Where is your operating system creating the most friction?

Friction shows up in predictable places:

Repeated collisions: Areas where you keep running into the same problems despite different circumstances. If similar conflicts keep arising with different people, the pattern is yours.

Energy drains: Activities that deplete you disproportionately - not because they're inherently difficult, but because your operating system makes them difficult. The task that should take an hour but somehow consumes your entire day.

Chronic gaps: The persistent space between what you know you should do and what you actually do. The feedback you keep getting but can't seem to act on. The change you've tried to make a dozen times.

Relationship patterns: Similar dynamics that keep appearing with different people. If everyone seems to have the same problem with you, they're seeing something you're not.

Identifying Your Highest-Leverage Development Areas

Not all friction points are equally important. Some patterns create minor inconvenience; others fundamentally limit your effectiveness. For each pattern you've identified, assess:

Cost: How much is this pattern costing you - in effectiveness, energy, relationships or results? A pattern that creates daily friction costs more than one that shows up occasionally.

Relevance: How central is this pattern to your current leadership challenges? A pattern that's blocking your biggest initiative matters more than one affecting peripheral work.

Readiness: How ready are you to do the work of changing it? Some patterns you're ready to face; others you're still defending. Readiness matters because forced change rarely sticks.

The highest-priority upgrades sit at the intersection of high cost, high relevance and genuine readiness. Trying to upgrade everything at once leads to upgrading nothing. Focus creates transformation.

Going Deeper: Formal Assessment

The diagnostic work in this chapter can surface significant insight. But if you've found yourself wanting more precision - clearer measurement, more specific patterns, a more comprehensive map - a formal assessment can provide it.

The Leaderwired™ Assessment was designed specifically to evaluate where you stand across all three dimensions the 7-5-3 Human Upgrade Code™:

Component Capacity: How developed is each of your seven operating system components? Where is your belief architecture creating friction? Which of your mindsets, emotional processing patterns, thought patterns, behavioral defaults, values, and communication protocols need attention?

Skillset Emergence: To what degree are the five premium skillsets showing up in your leadership? The assessment reveals which skillsets - cognitive flexibility, emotional intelligence at scale, human-AI collaboration design, strategic sensemaking, and exponential thinking - are emerging naturally and which are being blocked by OS limitations.

Foundation Strength: How solid are the three cultural foundations - Curiosity, Care, and Courage - that enable your transformation to scale? These determine whether your upgrade becomes collective capacity or stays individual.

The Leaderwired™ Assessment is available at [www.Leaderwired.com]. It makes visible what self-reflection alone cannot: the hidden architecture of your internal operating system.

Exercise: Creating Your Operating System Map

Before moving to Part Two, take time to create a concrete map of your current operating system. This isn't just reflection, it's the foundation for all the work that follows.

For each of the seven components, write:

1. One pattern that serves you well - a strength to leverage
2. One pattern that creates friction - a limitation to address
3. One question you're curious to explore

Then identify your top three upgrade priorities, the patterns where change would create the most significant positive impact on your leadership. This map will be your guide through the chapters ahead. Return to it as you work through each component. Update it as you gain new insights. The map isn't static, it evolves as you do.

From Diagnosis to Development

The diagnostic work you've done here isn't just preparation, it's the beginning of transformation. Awareness itself begins to shift patterns. Once you can see your operating system, you can never unsee it.

You'll notice your beliefs activating in real time - the anxiety when you don't have an answer, the urge to control, the impulse to bypass emotion. You'll catch your mindsets orienting - toward certainty or curiosity, toward control or orchestration. You'll feel your defaults executing, and in that feeling, find the space for choice.

That noticing is the first step toward choice. And choice is the first step toward change.

But awareness alone isn't enough. The chapters that follow will take you deep into each component, providing the methodology for upgrade.

David, the technology VP who discovered he wasn't really listening, did this work. It took months. He had to rebuild his relationship with his team, earning back the trust that his performance of consultation had eroded. He had to learn to ask questions he genuinely didn't know the answer to, and to tolerate the vulnerability that came with not-knowing.

"The hardest part wasn't changing the behavior," he told me later. "It was accepting that the story I'd been telling myself about who I was as a leader... wasn't the story other people were experiencing. I had to grieve that version of myself before I could build a new one."

That grief is part of the upgrade process. The old operating system served you, it deserves acknowledgment even as you release it. The patterns that created friction were also the patterns that got you here. Honoring that complexity makes change possible.

You've now diagnosed where your operating system needs attention. You've identified your friction points and your highest-leverage development opportunities. You have a map.

Part Two begins the upgrade work itself - component by component, pattern by pattern, building the internal architecture that AI-era leadership requires.

The map is in your hands. Now it's time to begin the journey.

∽

END OF PART ONE

INTERNAL ARCHITECTURE

Upgrading the Seven Components

BELIEF ARCHITECTURE

THE FOUNDATION THAT SHAPES EVERYTHING ELSE

Alison knew she should speak up. The CEO had just asked for perspectives on the restructuring plan, and she had spent three weeks analyzing exactly this scenario. Her insights were sharp. Her data was solid. The room was waiting.

She opened her mouth - and watched herself close it again.

The Chief Strategy Officer filled the silence with a point she'd been about to make. Then the CFO added context she'd already prepared. The conversation moved on. When it was over, the CEO thanked everyone for their input. Alison had contributed nothing.

In the elevator afterward, her colleague turned to her. "I thought you had something on that. Your analysis was better than what got said in there."

"I know," Alison said. And she did know. That was the worst part.

This wasn't stage fright. Alison was a Global Marketing Director at a Fortune 100 company, leading teams across three continents, driving campaigns that generated hundreds of millions in revenue. She presented to boards, negotiated with executives, and commanded rooms full of stakeholders. On paper, she had achieved extraordinary success.

But something kept stopping her. Every time an opportunity emerged to step into a bigger role, to advocate more forcefully for her ideas, to take a risk that might expose her to failure - something would intervene. Not fear exactly, but something quieter. A deep conviction, running beneath conscious awareness, that she wasn't quite enough.

"The beliefs weren't dramatic or easily named," she told me later. "They were more like background assumptions - quiet rules about what was possible for someone like me, what I deserved, how visible I could safely become."

These beliefs hadn't arrived through conscious choice. They had been installed gradually, through years of subtle messages, early experiences, and self-protective adaptations that had once served a purpose. And because they had been running for so long, they didn't feel like beliefs at all.

They felt like reality.

That moment in the executive meeting - watching herself stay silent when she had something valuable to say - became Alison's wake-up call. The ceiling she'd been pressing against for years wasn't external. It was architectural. And architecture can be rebuilt.

The Architecture Beneath Everything

Your belief architecture is the foundational layer of your operating system - the bedrock assumptions about yourself, others, and how the world works that filter every piece of information you receive and shape every response you generate. These aren't surface-level opinions you could easily articulate if asked. They're deeper structures, operating mostly beneath conscious awareness, that determine what you notice, what you ignore, what seems possible, and what feels impossible.

If you've driven for years, think about what happens when you approach a green light. You don't consciously think "green means safe to proceed" - you just go. That belief was installed through repetition until it became automatic, running beneath awareness. Now imagine someone rewired the system overnight: red means go, green means stop. Your conscious mind might know the new rules, but your foot would still hesitate at green, still twitch toward the brake at red. That's the power of encoded beliefs - they run faster than conscious thought, and knowing better doesn't automatically change them.

Your beliefs about traffic lights are low stakes. Your beliefs about leadership - about what makes you credible, about whether vulnerability is safe, about what you're capable of - run just as automatically, with far greater consequences.

Consider how this works in practice. A leader who believes "I must have all the answers to be respected" will experience a knowledge gap as threatening. She'll avoid situations where she might appear uncertain. She'll feel compelled to provide solutions even when asking questions would be more effective. She doesn't consciously think these things in the moment - the belief just runs, filtering reality and generating responses automatically, so quickly she doesn't even notice it happening.

This is both the power and the problem of belief architecture. Beliefs that serve you - "I can learn anything I need to learn," "People generally want to do good work," "Challenges make me stronger" - create upward spirals of effectiveness and wellbeing. Beliefs that limit you create the opposite: downward spirals where your beliefs generate behaviors that produce outcomes that confirm the original beliefs, tightening the grip of limitation with each cycle.

AI-era implication: When AI can provide answers faster than any human, the belief that "I must have all the answers" becomes catastrophically limiting. Leaders who can't update this belief will either resist AI as a threat to their identity or be paralyzed by it. The upgrade: "My value comes from asking better questions, not from having better answers." This reframe doesn't diminish your value, it repositions it to where human capability remains essential.

What's Running Beneath Your Awareness?

Before we go further, pause. Think about a recent situation where you held back—where you had something to contribute but didn't, where you knew what you should do but couldn't make yourself do it, where you watched yourself behave in ways that didn't serve you.

What was the quiet voice in that moment? Not the loud fears, but the background assumption? "They won't take me seriously." "I might be wrong." "This isn't my place." "I should wait until I'm more certain."

That voice is your belief architecture speaking. And it's been speaking for a long time - so long that you probably don't hear it as a voice anymore. You hear it as truth.

Hold that voice in mind as you read this chapter. We're going to examine how these beliefs form, why they persist, and how they can be rebuilt.

The Limiting Beliefs That Hold Leaders Back

In nearly two decades of working with executives across industries, I've encountered certain limiting beliefs with striking regularity. They appear in different forms and intensities, but their core patterns are remarkably consistent.

I'll explore four of these beliefs in depth - the ones I see creating the most friction in the AI era - and then briefly introduce three others you should watch for.

"I Must Have All the Answers"

This belief equates leadership authority with certainty and expertise. Leaders who hold it experience not-knowing as a threat to their identity and credibility. They feel compelled to provide answers even in ambiguous situations, struggle to say "I don't know" and become defensive when their knowledge is challenged.

David, VP I worked with, realized this belief was sabotaging his AI initiative. His team had stopped bringing him problems because he always jumped to solutions - solutions that weren't informed by the frontline reality they were experiencing.

"I thought being helpful meant having answers," he reflected. "I didn't realize that my answers were actually shutting down the learning we needed. Every time I jumped in with a solution, I was signaling that my knowing mattered more than their discovering. Eventually, they stopped discovering anything - they just waited for me to tell them what to do."

This belief often originates in early career success built on technical expertise. Having answers was how these leaders proved their value, earned promotions and built reputations. The belief served them well

- until they reached levels where the right answer is rarely clear, where admitting uncertainty is strength, and where the job is to facilitate collective intelligence rather than provide individual solutions.

AI-era cost: AI can generate answers faster than you can think. If your value depends on having answers, you're competing with systems that will always outpace you. The leaders who thrive will be those who ask questions AI can't formulate and make judgments AI can't make. Your competitive advantage shifts from knowledge to wisdom, from answers to questions, from providing certainty to navigating uncertainty.

"If I Don't Do It, Who Will?"

This belief - which we saw in Marcus's story - drives leaders to take on everything themselves. It shows up as difficulty delegating, an inability to trust others with important work, and a pattern of stepping in rather than stepping back. The leader becomes indispensable, which sounds like success but is actually a trap.

Marcus traced his version back to being twelve years old, caring for his siblings while his father was sick and his mother worked two jobs. In that context, the belief was accurate - if he didn't handle things, they genuinely wouldn't get handled. The belief saved his family.

But thirty years later, leading a thriving firm, the same belief was creating exactly what he feared: a team that couldn't function without him. His hovering, checking, and correcting actually undermined team capability by preventing the learning that comes from ownership and autonomy. The belief that protected his family was now suffocating his organization.

Related beliefs cluster around this one: "Asking for help is weakness." "I can't trust others to follow through." "Quality requires my involvement." Each variation drives the same pattern of over-functioning that exhausts the leader and under-develops the team.

AI-era cost: AI implementation requires letting go. You can't personally review every AI-assisted decision. You can't maintain control over systems that operate at machine speed. The belief that you must do it yourself will make you the constraint on your organization's AI adoption - and eventually, its survival.

"I Can't Make Mistakes"

Perfectionism in leadership shows up as paralysis in the face of ambiguity, endless analysis before decisions, and an inability to move forward without certainty. Leaders with this belief often drive their teams toward the same impossible standard, creating cultures where risk-taking is suppressed and innovation dies before it can take root.

One executive described the exhausting mental gymnastics this belief required: "I would run every possible scenario, trying to guarantee the outcome before I committed. By the time I was ready to decide, the opportunity had usually passed. And then I'd criticize myself for missing it - another mistake, another confirmation that I wasn't good enough."

Notice the trap: the fear of mistakes leads to delay, delay leads to missed opportunities, missed opportunities feel like mistakes, which reinforces the fear. The belief creates the very outcome it's trying to prevent.

The fear of mistakes typically connects to deeper beliefs about self-worth being contingent on performance. A mistake doesn't just mean a setback - it means something about who the leader is as a person. The stakes of any decision become existential, which makes deciding almost impossible.

AI-era cost: AI integration requires experimentation, and experimentation means mistakes. Organizations that learn fastest will be those that try things, fail quickly, and adjust. Adopt a "Fail small, Scale big" mentality. Leaders who can't tolerate mistakes will watch their organizations fall behind while more experimental competitors learn their way forward.

"I Don't Belong Here"

This was Alison's belief - and it's one of the most common I encounter. Imposter syndrome appears at every level, including the C-suite. Leaders with this belief doubt their right to be in the room, second-guess their contributions, and hold back from full visibility. The quiet insecurity limits their impact far more than any actual capability gap.

The belief is particularly insidious because it's self-concealing. Leaders experiencing it rarely talk about it - after all, admitting to imposter feelings risks confirming that they're indeed imposters. They suffer in silence while their potential remains unrealized and their organizations miss the full contribution they could make.

What makes this belief especially cruel is that high achievers are often most susceptible to it. The very drive that got them to senior levels can fuel the sense that they haven't really earned their place - that they've somehow fooled everyone, and eventually the truth will come out.

AI-era cost: AI will challenge everyone's expertise. If you already doubt whether you belong, AI's capabilities can trigger a crisis of identity. The upgrade: your value isn't in what you know but in the uniquely human judgment you bring—judgment that becomes more valuable, not less, as AI handles routine knowledge work.

Which of These Do You Recognize?

Pause here. Of the four beliefs we've explored, which ones create friction in your leadership?

Most leaders carry some version of multiple beliefs. The question isn't whether you have them - you do, we all do. The question is which ones are currently costing you the most.

Think about your friction points from Chapter 3. What beliefs might be generating those patterns?

Three More Beliefs to Watch For

"Others should perform like I do." This belief leads to unrealistic expectations and chronic disappointment in team members. It misses a fundamental truth: your job isn't to clone yourself but to build teams where diverse capabilities combine to produce results no individual could achieve alone. In the AI era, this belief becomes especially costly - AI will perform differently than humans, and leaders who expect AI to think like they do will either over-trust it or under-trust it.

"I can't say no." Leaders with this belief spread themselves impossibly thin, taking on too many commitments and blurring priorities. The irony: saying yes to everything means saying yes to the wrong things. Strategic leadership requires the discipline to decline what's unimportant. In the AI era, with endless new possibilities to evaluate, leaders who can't say no will be overwhelmed by optionality.

"Asking for help is weakness." This belief frames self-sufficiency as strength and interdependence as inadequacy. The cost is twofold: the leader becomes a bottleneck and burnout risk, while the team is denied growth opportunities. Leaders who grew up in environments where resources were scarce often carry this belief - what protected you then may be limiting you now. The AI era will require an abundance mentality to maximize outcomes.

How Limiting Beliefs Get Built

Understanding how beliefs form helps demystify them. When you see the construction process, beliefs lose some of their power to masquerade as unchangeable facts.

Let's trace Marcus's belief through its formation:

Early experience installed the foundation. At twelve, Marcus learned that when things needed doing, he had to do them. His father was sick. His mother was working two jobs. If he didn't handle things at home, they wouldn't get handled. This wasn't a belief he chose - it was a survival adaptation that encoded itself into his operating system.

Repetition reinforced the structure. Every time Marcus stepped up and things worked out, the belief strengthened. The neural pathway became more efficient. What started as an interpretation - "I need to handle this" - became an assumption, then a conviction, then an invisible filter on reality that felt like the way things simply are.

Success confirmed the system. During the 2008 financial crisis, Marcus's "I'll handle it" approach saved his firm. That success became armor, protecting the belief from examination. "My approach got us through 2008" made it harder to see how the same approach might be creating problems in 2024. Past success is the most effective defense a limiting belief can have.

Identity integrated the belief. Eventually, the belief became part of how Marcus defined himself. "I'm someone who handles things.

I'm the one people count on. That's just who I am." At this stage, challenging the belief felt like challenging his identity - existentially threatening rather than merely uncomfortable.

This is the construction process for every limiting belief. Yours followed a similar path - from early adaptation to reinforced pattern to success-confirmed conviction to identity-integrated "truth." Seeing the construction doesn't dissolve the belief, but it opens space for deconstruction.

The Upgrade Process

Beliefs that took decades to build won't dissolve overnight. But they can be systematically examined and gradually replaced. The process involves four stages:

Stage 1: Surface the Belief

You can't upgrade what you can't see. The first step is making implicit beliefs explicit - bringing them from the shadows of automatic operation into the light of conscious awareness.

Start by examining your friction points. Where do you keep getting stuck despite your best efforts? What situations trigger disproportionate anxiety or defensiveness? What feedback have you received repeatedly but struggled to act on?

Behind each friction point is usually a limiting belief. The leader who can't delegate effectively often believes she must do things herself. The executive who avoids difficult conversations often believes conflict is dangerous. The manager who works himself to exhaustion often believes his value depends on his output.

Exercise: Think of a recurring challenge in your leadership - something that keeps appearing despite your efforts to address it. Write down three beliefs that might be contributing to the pattern. Don't censor yourself; just notice what arises.

Stage 2: Trace the Origin

Once a belief is surfaced, trace it back. Where did it come from? When did you first learn to think this way? What experiences reinforced it?

This isn't about assigning blame or dwelling in the past. It's about understanding that beliefs are constructed, not given. A belief that was installed at age eight in response to a specific situation isn't necessarily true for a forty-five-year-old leader facing different challenges. Seeing the construction demystifies the belief and opens space for reconstruction.

When Marcus traced his belief back to his childhood, the belief lost some of its grip. It was still there, still powerful, but now he could see it as an adaptation to a specific situation rather than a fundamental truth about leadership or about himself.

Stage 3: Test the Accuracy

Most limiting beliefs contain a grain of truth that's been over-generalized. The work is to find the boundaries - where is this belief accurate, and where does it create unnecessary limitation?

The test questions:

Is this belief absolutely true in all circumstances?

What evidence contradicts it?

What would someone who doesn't hold this belief do differently?

What's the cost of continuing to operate from this belief?

What might become possible if this belief were updated?

Stage 4: Install the Alternative

The brain doesn't do well with voids. Removing a limiting belief without replacing it leaves a vacuum that the old pattern will rush to fill. The final stage is deliberately installing an alternative belief - one that serves your current reality better.

The alternative shouldn't be the opposite extreme. If your limiting belief is "I must have all the answers," the upgrade isn't "I should never provide answers." It's something more nuanced: "My value comes from facilitating good decisions, which sometimes means providing answers and sometimes means asking questions." This alternative is both more accurate and more useful.

Installation happens through repetition and evidence. State the new belief regularly. Look for evidence that supports it. Act from it even when the old belief pulls you back. Over time, the new belief builds its own neural pathway, becoming more automatic while the old pathway weakens from disuse.

Behavioral Experiments: Testing New Beliefs Through Action

Intellectual understanding isn't enough to change beliefs. You have to test new beliefs through action, gathering evidence that the brain can't dismiss.

Jackie held the belief "Admitting uncertainty will undermine my authority." She'd built her career on being the person with answers. When she didn't know something, she either delayed until she figured it out or gave a confident response that was less informed than it appeared.

The experiment: In her next leadership team meeting, when asked about the timeline for an AI implementation she genuinely wasn't sure about, she would say "I don't know yet" and then ask for input.

"I was terrified," she told me later. "I literally rehearsed the words in my head. 'I don't know yet.' Four words. It shouldn't be that hard."

What happened surprised her. When she said "I don't know yet - what are you all seeing from your teams?", the room shifted. Her Chief Medical Officer shared concerns he'd been holding back. Her HR director raised implementation challenges she'd been trying to solve alone. The conversation became more substantive than any they'd had in months.

"They didn't lose respect for me," Jackie reflected. "They actually seemed relieved. Like I'd given them permission to not have all the answers either."

One experiment didn't dissolve Jackie's belief, but it created a crack. She had evidence now - concrete, lived evidence - that uncertainty could create connection rather than undermine authority. That evidence made the next experiment easier. And the next.

Design your experiment: Identify one limiting belief you're ready to test. What small action would challenge it? Not the biggest, most consequential situation - start with something meaningful but not catastrophic if it goes wrong. Then run the experiment and observe: What actually happened? Was your fear realized? What did you learn?

The AI-Era Belief Audit

Beyond the universal limiting beliefs, AI creates specific belief challenges that deserve examination:

"AI will replace me." This fear-based belief creates either resistance (fighting AI to protect your role) or paralysis (unable to engage with something you've already decided will destroy you). *The upgrade:* "AI will change what I do, but uniquely human capabilities - judgment, creativity, emotional intelligence, ethical reasoning - become more valuable, not less."

"I need to understand AI technically before I can lead AI initiatives." This belief delays action indefinitely, since AI technical understanding is a moving target. Colin Powell's 40-70 Rule applies here: you need 40-70% of the information to decide well. Less than 40% is reckless; more than 70% means the opportunity has passed. Leaders waiting for complete AI understanding will wait forever. *The upgrade:* "I need to understand AI's capabilities and limitations well enough to make good decisions. That's different from technical expertise."

"My team will figure out AI on their own." This hands-off belief leaves teams without direction, resources, or permission to experiment. Leaders who hold it often frame it as empowerment, but teams experience it as abandonment - unclear on priorities, unsure if experimentation is truly welcomed, and left to navigate transformation without support. *The upgrade:* "AI adoption requires leadership - setting direction, encouraging experimentation and making resource decisions."

"AI is just another tool." This belief leads to underinvestment in the organizational changes AI requires. Leaders who hold it implement AI like they'd implement new software - without rethinking the processes, skills, and structures that need to change alongside it. *The upgrade*: "AI is a transformation, not a tool. It requires rethinking how we work, not just what tools we use."

From Architecture to Action

Your belief architecture is powerful, but not permanent. It was built through experience, and it can be rebuilt through experience. The process requires attention, method, and practice - but it's entirely possible.

Alison did this work. Within eighteen months of that executive meeting where she watched herself stay silent, she had stepped into a C-suite role she'd previously convinced herself was beyond her reach. The ceiling had been real - but it was internal, not external. And once she saw it clearly, she could rebuild it.

"She held the space and accountability for me to show up and do the work," Alison reflected on our coaching engagement. The shift happened, she said, "beautifully with compassion and wisdom." Not through willpower or positive thinking, but through systematic examination and deliberate rewiring.

That's what belief change requires: space to examine yourself honestly, and accountability to actually do something with what you discover. The space creates the conditions; the work creates the change.

The Connection to Mindsets

Beliefs are the foundation - but they don't operate alone. Built on top of your belief architecture is your mindset layer: the default orientations that determine how you approach challenges, uncertainty, and change.

Here's the connection: limiting beliefs create limiting mindsets. A leader who believes "I must have all the answers" will default to a certainty-seeking mindset rather than a curiosity mindset. A leader who believes "I can't make mistakes" will default to risk avoidance rather than experimentation.

When you upgrade your belief architecture, you create the conditions for mindset shifts. The foundation becomes stable enough to support new orientations. That's what we'll explore in the next chapter: the five mindset shifts that define AI-era leadership - and how upgraded beliefs make those shifts possible.

Your belief architecture is foundational - but not fixed. The foundation can be rebuilt. And when it is, everything built upon it becomes more solid, more stable, more capable of supporting the leadership you're growing into.

MINDSETS

THE FIVE UPGRADES THAT UNLOCK AI-ERA LEADERSHIP

The VP killed the proposal in forty-five seconds.

His team had spent three months developing an AI-powered product recommendation engine. The data was compelling - customer testing showed a thirty-two percent improvement in conversion rates. The technical architecture was sound. The business case projected significant revenue impact within two quarters.

But when they presented to David, the seasoned executive who had built his reputation on deep market intuition, he shut it down. "Our customers would never go for that," he said, pointing to his fifteen years of market experience. "I know this market. This isn't what they want."

Three months later, a competitor launched exactly that product. They captured eighteen percent market share in six weeks. David's certainty had cost his organization a significant competitive opportunity.

What cost David wasn't a lack of experience, it was refusing to investigate data that contradicted his experience. His certainty, the very quality that had built his career, became the blind spot that undermined his judgment. He couldn't see what he couldn't see, because his mindset prevented him from even looking.

This is the mindset trap. The mental orientations that powered your rise to leadership can become the very obstacles that prevent you from leading effectively at the next level. The certainty that made you decisive becomes rigidity. The control that made you reliable becomes micromanagement. The expertise that made you authoritative becomes an inability to learn.

What follows are five critical mindset upgrades - internal psychological shifts that form the foundation for everything that comes later in this book. Think of these as rewiring your mental operating system at the source code level.

In Part Four, you'll encounter the Five AI Leadership Shifts™ (Chapter 13) - the external pivots in how you lead with AI. But those external shifts are impossible without first doing this internal work. You cannot shift how you lead until you've upgraded how you think.

These upgrades don't replace your existing capabilities - they expand your range. The goal isn't to abandon certainty for curiosity, but to access either depending on what the situation requires. Mindset maturity isn't about which mode you default to - it's whether you can consciously choose.

Why Mindsets Matter Now

Organizations invest heavily in new technologies, new strategies, new structures - while leadership mindsets remain fundamentally unchanged. They're running sophisticated new programs on outdated mental operating systems. And then they wonder why transformation stalls.

The gap isn't technical, it's cognitive. We're asking leaders trained in certainty to embrace ambiguity. Leaders rewarded for control to enable autonomy. Leaders whose authority came from expertise to acknowledge what they don't know. The shift isn't just difficult; for many leaders, it feels like betraying the very approaches that made them successful.

Three forces make this cognitive gap more consequential than ever:

Accelerating change. AI capabilities increased 100x in power in 2025 while leadership models remain static. Market conditions shift faster than planning cycles can accommodate. The half-life of specific knowledge is measured in months, not years.

Expanding ambiguity. Clear playbooks are increasingly rare. Unlike previous eras where best practices could be identified and replicated, today's challenges often lack proven solutions.

Complexity of collaboration. Human-AI collaboration requires fundamentally rethinking decision authority, quality control and value creation.

Upgrade One: From Certainty to Curiosity

Traditional leadership valued decisive certainty. Today's challenges increasingly don't match historical patterns. The upgrade isn't from certainty to uncertainty - it's from certainty to curiosity. Curiosity maintains forward motion while remaining open to new information.

The Old Pattern: "I've seen this before. I know what to do."

The Upgraded Pattern: "This looks familiar but let me verify what's actually different. What might I be missing?"

Upgrade Two: From Control to Orchestration

The volume and velocity of decisions has exceeded any individual's capacity. Orchestration means designing systems where the right decisions get made by the right people at the right time - without requiring your direct involvement in each one.

The Old Pattern: "I need to review this before we move forward."

The Upgraded Pattern: "Here's the framework for making this type of decision. You have authority to decide within these parameters."

Upgrade Three: From Expertise to Learning Velocity

Expertise still matters, but its half-life has shortened dramatically. The sustainable advantage isn't in what you know, it's in how fast you can learn what you don't know.

The Old Pattern: "I've spent twenty years mastering this field. That expertise is my value."

The Upgraded Pattern: "My ability to learn quickly as the field evolves is what keeps me valuable."

Upgrade Four: From Risk Avoidance to Experimentation

The cost of not experimenting now exceeds the cost of failed experiments. Experimentation treats failure as data rather than disaster.

The Old Pattern: "We need more data before we commit to this approach."

The Upgraded Pattern: "Let's design a small experiment to generate the data we need."

Upgrade Five: From Individual Decisions to Collaborative Intelligence

Collaborative intelligence means decisions emerging from collective input rather than individual judgment - designing systems where diverse perspectives integrate efficiently.

The Old Pattern: "All final decisions come through me."

The Upgraded Pattern: "We've defined which decisions need my judgment, which benefit from AI augmentation, and which the team owns completely."

The Upgrades as a System

These five upgrades don't operate in isolation. They form an interconnected system where each mindset upgrade supports and enables the others.

Curiosity enables learning velocity - you can't learn quickly if you're not curious about what you don't know. Learning velocity enables experimentation - the faster you learn, the more willing you are to run experiments that might fail. Experimentation enables orchestration - as you learn what works, you can build better frameworks for others to follow. Orchestration enables collaborative intelligence - when you're not controlling everything, others can contribute more fully.

The Integration Challenge

Each mindset upgrade involves letting go of something that once served you. Certainty provided confidence. Control provided security. Expertise provided identity. Risk avoidance provided safety. Individual decision-making provided clarity.

The upgrade isn't about abandoning these entirely, it's about expanding your range. The goal is to access certainty when it serves you and curiosity when it serves better. The measure of mindset maturity isn't which mode you default to, it's whether you can consciously choose based on context.

The Bridge to AI Leadership

These five mindset upgrades prepare your internal operating system for a larger transformation. In Part Four, after you've upgraded all seven components, developed the five emerging skillsets and built the three cultural foundations, we'll return to these themes in a new context: leading AI transformation at scale.

You'll see how the internal work you're doing now translates into external leadership practice. How "Certainty to Curiosity" as a mindset upgrade enables "AI as Threat to AI as Amplifier" as a leadership shift. How "Control to Orchestration" internally enables "AI Implementation to AI Integration" externally.

The upgrades are the foundation. The shifts are the application. Both are essential to the complete 7-5-3 Human Upgrade Code™.

But first, there's more internal work to do. The mindset component is just one of seven. Let's continue with the next component of your operating system: emotional processing.

EMOTIONAL PROCESSING

The Hidden Capacity That Determines How You Lead Under Pressure

The 360-degree feedback report had just arrived.

David, the technology VP we've followed through this book, opened it expecting confirmation. He'd been a high performer for twelve years, promoted twice, consistently rated as exceeding expectations. He knew who he was as a leader. The feedback would reflect that.

The first page was fine. Strong scores on strategic thinking, technical expertise, drive for results. Then he turned to the verbatim comments.

"David doesn't listen. He's already made up his mind before meetings start."

"People have stopped bringing him ideas because he makes them feel stupid for suggesting anything he hasn't already thought of."

"His questions aren't questions. They're tests to see if you'll agree with him."

In the next thirty seconds, a cascade of responses flooded through David's nervous system. Heat rising in his face. Jaw clenching. Heart rate accelerating. Thoughts fragmenting into defenses, accusations, counterarguments. His body was preparing for threat—mobilizing resources to fight back against danger that existed only in words on his screen.

"That can't be right," he said aloud, to no one.

What happened next would determine more than just how David felt. It would shape whether he could learn from this feedback or dismiss it, whether his relationships with his team would improve or deteriorate further, whether his leadership would evolve or calcify.

This is the moment where emotional processing capacity shows up - or doesn't.

Why This Chapter Follows Mindsets

In Chapter 5, we explored the mindset shifts that AI-era leadership requires: from certainty to curiosity, from control to orchestration, from expertise to learning velocity. These shifts are essential - but they're also emotionally demanding.

Moving from certainty to curiosity requires tolerating the anxiety of not knowing. Moving from control to orchestration requires tolerating the fear that something will go wrong without you. Moving from expertise to learning velocity requires tolerating the vulnerability of being a beginner again.

Each mindset shift asks you to sit with emotions that your old operating system was designed to avoid. And if you can't process those emotions - if they overwhelm you, if you suppress them, if they drive you back to old patterns - the mindset shifts won't stick.

David couldn't shift from certainty to curiosity until he could process the emotional devastation of discovering that his self-perception was wrong. The feedback didn't just challenge his behavior, it challenged his identity. And identity threats trigger the most powerful emotional responses we have.

Most leadership development ignores this moment. We teach strategy, communication and decision-making, but we don't teach the foundational capacity that determines whether any of those skills are accessible when you need them most.

What Emotional Processing Actually Means

Emotional processing isn't about suppressing emotions or expressing them freely. It's about having the internal capacity to experience emotions fully without being hijacked by them - to let feelings inform your leadership without controlling it.

Think of it as the difference between *having* emotions and being *had* by them. A leader with strong emotional processing capacity can notice rising frustration and use that information to understand what matters - without the frustration taking over and dictating behavior. A leader with weak capacity is taken over by the frustration, unable to think clearly or choose their response deliberately.

Research from the Center for Creative Leadership reveals that seventy-five percent of executive derailments stem from poor emotional regulation - not lack of intelligence, not lack of technical skill, but inability to manage emotional responses under pressure. The executives who fail often fail because their emotional processing breaks down in critical moments.

AI-era implication: AI implementation creates intense emotional challenges - threat responses to AI capability, anxiety about uncertainty, grief over changing roles, responsibility for decisions that affect people's livelihoods. Leaders whose emotional processing is compromised can't navigate these challenges or help their teams navigate them. They transmit anxiety rather than providing the steady presence that transformation requires.

Your Emotional Processing Patterns

Before we go further, consider your own patterns.

When was the last time you were emotionally hijacked at work? Not mildly irritated - truly hijacked, where you said or did something you later regretted, or where you couldn't think clearly because the emotion was too intense?

What triggered it? A criticism? A perceived injustice? A threat to something you'd invested in? A challenge to your competence or identity?

What did you do? Did you react immediately? Withdraw? Suppress it and have it leak out later? Ruminate for hours or days?

Hold that memory as you read this chapter. We're going to examine how these patterns form, why they persist, and how they can be upgraded.

The Nervous System Foundation

Your emotional processing capacity is rooted in your nervous system. Understanding this biology isn't just academic - it's practical. When you know how your nervous system works, you can intervene more effectively when it's not serving you.

Stephen Porges's polyvagal theory describes three states your nervous system can occupy:

Social engagement: When you feel safe, your nervous system supports connection, creativity and clear thinking. This is the state where you can access your full capabilities as a leader - where you can think strategically, communicate effectively and build relationships.

Fight or flight: When you perceive threat, your nervous system mobilizes for defense. Heart rate increases, stress hormones flood your system, and your thinking narrows to threat-focused processing. This state was designed for physical danger, but it activates for psychological threats too, like feedback that challenges your identity.

Shutdown: When threat seems overwhelming, your nervous system can move into conservation mode - numbing, disconnecting, withdrawing. This is less common in leadership contexts but can show up as emotional flatness or disengagement under prolonged stress.

The key insight: your nervous system doesn't distinguish between physical threats and psychological ones. A devastating piece of feedback, a public challenge to your competence, or discovering that your self-perception is wrong triggers the same cascade as a predator would have for your ancestors. And once you're in threat response, your leadership capabilities are compromised - regardless of how skilled you are when you're calm.

What Gets Encoded

Your emotional processing patterns were largely established before you had any say in the matter. Early experiences taught your nervous system what was safe and what was dangerous. These lessons became encoded - automatic responses that run without conscious involvement.

Remember Marcus, whose "if I don't do it, who will" belief traced back to being twelve years old with a sick father? That wasn't just a belief that got encoded - it was an entire emotional pattern. The anxiety that arose when things weren't handled. The compulsion to step in. The inability to tolerate the discomfort of uncertainty about whether someone else would follow through.

At twelve, those emotional responses made sense. They drove behaviors that kept his family functioning. But thirty years later, the same emotional patterns were still running - still generating anxiety when he wasn't involved, still compelling him to take over, still making delegation feel viscerally unsafe.

This is how encoding works. A child who learned that expressing anger resulted in withdrawal of love learns to suppress anger. Decades later, that same person - now an executive - struggles to give direct feedback because anger still triggers fear of abandonment. The adult mind knows the situation is different. The nervous system runs out of the old pattern anyway.

A young professional who was publicly humiliated for a mistake learns to treat visibility as danger. Years later, that same person - now a senior leader, avoids high-profile opportunities that could advance their career. The reasoning is always something else, "I prefer behind-the-scenes work", but the pattern was installed in an earlier context.

These encoded patterns aren't weaknesses, they're adaptations that once served a purpose. The problem is that they run automatically, without checking whether the original danger still applies.

The Amygdala Hijack

Daniel Goleman popularized the term "amygdala hijack" to describe what happens when your threat-detection system takes over before your rational brain can intervene. The amygdala can trigger defensive responses in milliseconds, far faster than your executive brain can evaluate whether the threat is real.

When David read those 360 feedback comments, his amygdala detected identity threat and began mobilizing his nervous system before he'd even finished processing the words. By the time his rational brain could assess the situation, his body was already in threat response - heart pounding, face flushing, mind racing to construct defenses.

This isn't a design flaw, it's a survival feature. When threats were physical and immediate, you needed to respond before you could think. The problem is that this same system activates for modern threats that require thoughtful response rather than immediate reaction. The feedback report isn't going to attack David, but his nervous system doesn't know that.

The practice isn't eliminating the hijack - that's not possible given how your brain is wired. The practice is shortening recovery time and creating space for conscious choice before you do something you'll regret.

The Three-Second Gap

Between stimulus and response, there's a gap. For most people, that gap is about three seconds - the time it takes for your executive brain to come back online after an amygdala hijack begins. What you do with those three seconds determines whether you respond or react.

The practices that follow are all designed to expand this gap, to create more space between what happens and what you do about it. Not so you can suppress your emotions, but so you can choose how to express them in ways that serve your leadership.

Practice 1: The Physiological Reset

When your nervous system is activated, you can't think your way back to calm. You have to work with your body. The fastest interventions are physiological:

Extended exhale breathing. When you exhale longer than you inhale, you activate the parasympathetic nervous system - the "rest and digest" mode that counteracts threat response. Try breathing in for four counts and out for eight counts, three to five times. Simple, but remarkably effective.

Cold water. Splashing cold water on your face activates the diving reflex, which slows your heart rate. This sounds almost too simple to work, but it does - and it works fast.

Physical movement. Stress hormones prepare your body for action. Moving - even briefly - helps metabolize those hormones. A quick walk, some stretches, even tensing and releasing major muscle groups can shift your state.

Practice 2: The Naming Intervention

Neuroscience research shows that simply naming an emotion reduces its intensity. When you put words to what you're feeling, you shift activity from the reactive amygdala to the more regulated prefrontal cortex, aka "executive brain".

The practice is simple but requires building the habit. When you notice emotional activation, pause and name it specifically. Not "I feel bad" but "I feel anxious about losing credibility" or "I feel angry that my work was dismissed without discussion."

Granularity matters. Research shows that people with more nuanced emotional vocabulary have better emotional regulation. The difference between "angry" and "frustrated, disappointed, and a little scared" matters. Developing a richer palette of emotional words gives you more precise tools for the naming intervention.

Practice 3: The Perspective Shift

When you're emotionally activated, your attention narrows to the threat. Everything else fades. The perspective shift practice deliberately widens the aperture:

What will this matter in a week? In a year? In five years?

What aspects of this situation am I not seeing right now?

How would someone I respect handle this?

What's the most generous interpretation of the other person's behavior?

These questions work by engaging your prefrontal cortex - pulling your brain out of threat processing and into more balanced evaluation.

Building the Capacity Before You Need It

These practices only work under pressure if you've practiced them when pressure is low.

Jackie, the healthcare COO from Chapter 1, learned this the hard way. In her early coaching work, she understood the concepts intellectually. She could explain the three-second gap and recite the practices. But when she was actually triggered - when a board member questioned her judgment publicly, when a direct report's mistake threatened a major initiative - the practices vanished. Her nervous system took over, and she reacted from old patterns.

The breakthrough came when she started practicing in low-stakes situations. A mildly frustrating email - instead of firing back, she'd take three extended exhale breaths and name what she was feeling. A minor disagreement in a meeting - instead of pushing her point, she'd ask herself what she might not be seeing. A small disappointment - instead of powering through, she'd acknowledge the emotion and let it inform her response.

"It felt ridiculous at first," she told me. "These tiny moments didn't seem worth the effort. But I was building a new muscle. Every time I practiced the intervention in a small moment, I was making it more available for a big moment."

Six months later, when a genuinely significant crisis hit - a data breach that threatened patient trust and regulatory standing - Jackie found herself reaching for the practices automatically. Not because she was calm, but because she'd trained her nervous system to respond differently even when she wasn't calm.

"I was terrified," she said. "My heart was pounding. But somewhere in those first few seconds, I caught myself. I took the breaths. I named what I was feeling: scared, responsible, embarrassed. And then I could think. I could lead. Not because the fear went away, but because I had space around it."

The Recovery Protocol

Even with good emotional processing skills, you'll sometimes get hijacked. The question isn't whether it will happen - it's how quickly you can recover and whether you can minimize damage in the interim.

Step 1: Notice the hijack. The earlier you catch it, the easier recovery is. Signs include: body tension, racing thoughts, narrowed focus, impulse to act immediately, certainty that you're right and others are wrong.

Step 2: Interrupt the pattern. Use a physiological reset - breathing, cold water, movement. Don't try to think your way out, work with your body first.

Step 3: Create space. If possible, delay your response. "I want to think about this before I respond" or "Let me get back to you tomorrow" buys you time to process. That time is worth protecting.

Step 4: Process before responding. Use the naming intervention and perspective shift. Journal if that helps. Talk to a trusted person. Let the emotion inform your response without dictating it.

Step 5: Choose your response. Once you've processed, decide deliberately how to proceed. What response serves your goals, your values and the relationship?

David's Recovery

Back to David and that 360 feedback report. He didn't handle it perfectly, but he eventually handled it well enough.

His first response wasn't skillful. He spent the rest of that day constructing defenses, finding reasons why the feedback was unfair or uninformed. He mentally catalogued evidence that contradicted what his team had said. He was mobilizing for battle against a threat to his identity.

That evening, still agitated, he went for a long run - not as a deliberate practice, but because he couldn't sit still. The physical movement helped metabolize some of the stress hormones. By the time he got home, his nervous system had settled enough so that he could think more clearly.

He tried naming what he was feeling. Not just "upset" but more specifically: humiliated that his self-perception was so wrong. Scared that maybe the feedback was accurate. Angry that people hadn't told him directly. Sad about the relationships that had apparently been damaged without his knowing.

The naming helped. Each emotion, once identified, felt slightly less overwhelming. He wasn't drowning in undifferentiated distress anymore - he was experiencing specific feelings that he could examine one at a time.

The perspective shift came harder. His first attempt - "What's the most generous interpretation of this feedback?" - produced only resentment.

In our next coaching session, I asked him a different question: "What if this feedback is a gift? What if knowing this gives you a chance to change something that was limiting you without your awareness?"

That reframe didn't make the pain disappear. But it opened a crack. If the feedback was information rather than attack, he could work with it. If the goal was improvement rather than defense, he could learn.

The same transformation we saw unfold in Chapter 5, where his certainty gradually gave way to curiosity. The mindset shift was real, but it was only possible because he'd first processed the emotional devastation that made it necessary.

Where Do You Need to Start?

Consider your own emotional processing capacity. Where are the gaps?

Do you struggle to notice when you've been hijacked - only realizing hours later that you weren't thinking clearly?

Do you notice the hijack but can't seem to interrupt it - you know you're reactive but can't stop?

Do you suppress emotions rather than process them - keeping a calm exterior while tension builds inside?

Do you process quickly in the moment but then ruminate for hours or days afterward?

Each pattern suggests a different starting point. If you can't notice hijacks, start with body awareness practices - learning to read your physiological signals. If you notice but can't interrupt, start with the physiological reset - working with your body when your mind can't help. If you suppress, start with the naming intervention - building the habit of acknowledging what you're feeling. If you ruminate, start with the perspective shift - practicing the questions that pull you out of repetitive loops.

The AI-Era Emotional Landscape

AI implementation creates specific emotional challenges that require strong processing capacity:

Threat response to AI capability. When AI can do things you've spent years mastering, it's natural to feel threatened. Leaders who can't process this threat response will either resist AI or become paralyzed by it. Neither of which serves their organizations.

Uncertainty anxiety. AI's implications are genuinely uncertain. Leaders who need certainty to feel safe will struggle. The upgrade is developing tolerance for ambiguity, the ability to act productively despite uncertainty.

Grief over changing roles. AI will change what leaders do. Some aspects of work you've enjoyed may become automated. Processing this grief, acknowledging the loss while finding new sources of meaning, is essential.

Responsibility weight. Decisions about AI implementation affect people's livelihoods and the organization's future. The weight of this responsibility can be emotionally overwhelming without adequate processing capacity.

Leaders who develop strong emotional processing capacity can navigate these challenges while helping their teams do the same. Leaders who can't process their own emotions will transmit anxiety throughout their organizations, exactly when steady leadership is most needed.

From Processing to Integration

The goal of emotional processing isn't to eliminate emotions, it's to integrate them into your leadership. Emotions carry information. Fear might signal a genuine risk worth examining. Anger might reveal a values violation worth addressing. Sadness might indicate a loss worth honoring.

Leaders with integrated emotional capacity don't suppress their feelings or get controlled by them. They use emotional information alongside rational analysis to make better decisions and build stronger relationships.

This integration takes time. You're rewiring patterns that may have been encoded for decades. But with consistent practice, emotional processing can shift from a struggle to a strength, from something that undermines your leadership to something that enhances it.

The Connection to Thought Patterns

Here's what David discovered in the days after receiving that feedback: emotional hijacks don't just affect how you feel, they distort how you think.

When he was in threat response, his thinking narrowed. He filtered for evidence that confirmed his defenses and filtered out evidence that challenged them. He catastrophized about what the feedback meant for his future. He attributed his team's behavior to their failings rather than considering his own contribution.

These weren't random distortions - they were systematic patterns. The same patterns that affect every leader when emotional processing is compromised. And they have names: confirmation bias, catastrophizing, fundamental attribution error.

Emotional processing creates the conditions for clear thinking. But it doesn't automatically produce clear thinking. The thought patterns themselves - the cognitive habits that filter reality and shape interpretation - need their own examination and upgrade.

That's where we turn next.

<hr>

THOUGHT PATTERNS

THE COGNITIVE HABITS THAT SHAPE YOUR LEADERSHIP REALITY

In the hours after reading his 360-degree feedback, David's mind constructed an elaborate defense.

The feedback couldn't be accurate. The people who'd said he didn't listen were the ones who never had anything useful to say anyway. The criticism about his questions being "tests" came from team members who couldn't handle being challenged. The pattern he was seeing wasn't about him, it was about them. Their insecurity. Their unwillingness to engage with rigorous thinking.

By that evening, David had mentally catalogued every piece of evidence that contradicted the feedback. He remembered times he'd changed his mind based on input. He recalled meetings where he'd asked genuine questions. He assembled a case for why the feedback was unfair, uninformed, or simply wrong!

What David didn't notice - couldn't notice, at first - was what his mind was doing. It was filtering. Selectively surfacing memories that supported his existing self-image. Discounting information that challenged it. Attributing the feedback to others' character flaws rather than examining his own behavior.

His emotional processing had been compromised, as we explored in Chapter 6. But that wasn't the only thing happening. His *thinking* was compromised too, running patterns that felt like clear reasoning but were actually systematic distortions.

This is the hidden cost of emotional hijack: it doesn't just affect how you feel. It warps how you think. And the distorted thinking feels completely rational. David wasn't aware he was filtering evidence or making attribution errors. He experienced himself as simply seeing the situation clearly.

That's the nature of thought patterns. They're invisible to the person running them.

The Patterns We All Run

In the past twenty-four hours, you've probably:

- Assumed you knew why someone behaved a certain way - and been wrong

- Filtered out information that contradicted what you already believed

- Projected a current trend into the future without accounting for change

- Overweighted recent events and underweighted base rates

- Attributed others' behavior to character and your own to circumstance

You're not alone. Every leader does this. Every human does. These aren't personal failings, they're features of how human cognition works. The brain takes shortcuts to process the overwhelming complexity of reality. Those shortcuts are efficient, but they're not always accurate.

Your thought patterns are the cognitive habits that shape how you process information, solve problems, and make meaning. They're the invisible filters between raw reality and your experience of it. And they're particularly consequential for leaders, whose interpretations shape decisions that affect others.

Which Patterns Do You Recognize?

Before we examine specific distortions, consider: Which of those patterns showed up for you recently?

When did you last assume you understood someone's motivation, only to discover you were wrong? When did you filter out information that didn't fit your existing view? When did you attribute a colleague's failure to their character while attributing your own similar failure to circumstances?

Hold those memories as you read this chapter. The patterns we'll explore aren't abstract, they're running in your leadership right now.

The Speed and Invisibility Problem

Thought patterns operate at remarkable speed. A thought arises, generates an emotional response, and triggers a behavioral reaction - all in milliseconds, often beneath conscious awareness. By the time you notice you're reacting, the pattern has already played out.

Consider what happens when a team member misses a deadline. Before you've consciously evaluated the situation, a thought pattern has already generated an interpretation. Maybe: "They're not taking this seriously!" Or: "Something must have gone wrong." Or: "I should have followed up more closely."

Each interpretation is plausible. Each leads to different emotional responses and different actions. And you didn't choose which pattern ran - it just ran, automatically, based on how your cognitive system has been trained by years of experience.

AI-era implication: AI amplifies whatever thought patterns you bring to it. If you filter for confirming information, AI can find evidence for almost anything you already believe. If you catastrophize, AI can generate detailed scenarios of doom. Your thought patterns determine whether AI is a tool for better thinking or an amplifier of cognitive distortion.

The Major Distortions

Science has identified dozens of systematic thinking errors. Here are the ones that most affect leadership - illustrated through leaders we've already met.

Confirmation Bias: David's Defense

David's response to his 360 feedback was a textbook case of confirmation bias: noticing information that confirms what you already believe and filtering out information that contradicts it.

He wasn't doing this consciously. His brain was doing it for him, helpfully reducing cognitive load by fitting new data into existing mental models. Every memory of listening well was surfaced. Every example of changing his mind was amplified. Meanwhile, the patterns his team described - the questions that weren't questions, the predetermined conclusions - were explained away, minimized, or attributed to others' failings.

For leaders, confirmation bias is particularly dangerous because people tend to bring you information that confirms your known views. They want to please you, not challenge you. The combination of your internal filter and others' external filter can create an echo chamber where disconfirming data never reaches you.

David's breakthrough came when I asked him to consider a different question. Not "Is this feedback accurate?" but "What if this feedback is accurate? What would that mean? What would I need to change?" The question itself began to crack the filter.

The upgrade: Actively seek disconfirming evidence. Ask: "What would change my mind?" Create psychological safety for people to challenge your views. Treat information that surprises you as especially valuable, it's getting through filters that usually block it.

Attribution Error: Marcus's Double Standard

When Marcus's team members failed to deliver, he knew exactly why: they weren't committed enough. They didn't care the way he cared. They lacked the drive that had made him successful. Character flaws, all of them.

But when Marcus himself missed something - a deadline, a detail, a relationship that needed attention - he had reasons. He was overextended. He had competing priorities. The organization had put impossible demands on him. Circumstances, every time.

This asymmetry is so consistent it has a name: the fundamental attribution error. When others fail, we attribute it to their character - they're lazy, incompetent, uncommitted. When we fail, we attribute it to circumstances - we had bad information, insufficient resources, impossible constraints.

For Marcus, this pattern reinforced his "if I don't do it, who will" belief. His team's failures proved they couldn't be trusted. His own failures proved the burden was too heavy for one person. Both interpretations led to the same conclusion: he had to do more himself.

The upgrade: When someone fails, ask: "What circumstances might explain this?" When you fail, ask: "What did I contribute to this outcome?" Deliberately counteract the default pattern. Marcus eventually learned to ask: "What did I do, or not do, that made it harder for them to succeed?"

Catastrophizing: Sarah's Spiral

Sarah, the technology executive whose analytical rigor had become paralysis, was a master catastrophizer. Give her any AI implementation risk, and her mind would trace it to organizational collapse within minutes.

A data quality issue became: "The AI will make bad recommendations, customers will lose trust, we'll lose market share, the board will lose confidence, and I'll be seen as the leader who destroyed the company's competitive position."

A vendor delay became: "We'll miss the market window, competitors will establish dominance, we'll never catch up, and the entire AI strategy will be viewed as a failure, my failure."

The catastrophizing felt like prudent risk assessment. Sarah experienced herself as the responsible one, the one who saw dangers others missed. What she didn't see was that her thinking had jumped from minor issue to worst-case conclusion, skipping all the moderate outcomes in between.

This pattern creates unnecessary suffering and can become self-fulfilling. Sarah's catastrophic projections made her hesitant to act, which created delays, which made some of her fears more likely to materialize.

The upgrade: When you notice catastrophic thinking, ask: "What's the most likely outcome?" Not best case, not worst case - most likely. Sarah learned to map the full range of possibilities and assign rough probabilities. The catastrophic outcome was usually less than ten percent likelihood. But her mind had been treating it as ninety percent.

Three More Patterns to Watch

Availability Heuristic. You judge probability based on how easily examples come to mind. Dramatic, recent, or emotionally charged events seem more likely than statistics warrant. This is why leaders often overweight the risks that make headlines and underweight the risks that kill quietly. A dramatic failure gets attention; a gradual decline gets ignored until it's too late. *The upgrade:* When assessing risk, ask: "What's the actual base rate?" Seek data rather than relying on what comes to mind easily.

Sunk Cost Fallacy. You continue investing in something because of what you've already invested, rather than based on future value. The project that should be cancelled continues because "we've already put so much into it." What's already spent is gone regardless of what you do next. *The upgrade:* Ask: "If I were starting fresh today, with no history, would I begin this?" The answer should drive your decision more than what's already been invested.

Negativity Bias. Negative information carries more weight than positive information. Criticism stings more than praise pleases. Threats get more attention than opportunities. For leaders, this means focusing disproportionately on problems while underweighting progress—creating cultures of threat-avoidance rather than opporttunity-seeking. *The upgrade:* Deliberately balance attention. For every problem you focus on, identify an opportunity. The balance won't be natural, you have to create it intentionally.

The Inner Critic

Beyond general cognitive patterns, most leaders carry a specific thought pattern that deserves attention: the inner critic. This is the voice that says you're not good enough, that your successes were luck, that failure is imminent, that others would reject you if they knew the truth.

Alison, the global marketing director from Chapter 4 who watched herself stay silent in that executive meeting, knew this voice intimately.

"No matter what I achieved, there was always a voice saying it wasn't enough," she told me. "That I'd gotten lucky. That eventually people would see through me."

She had built an extraordinarily successful career - Fortune 100 company, global teams, campaigns generating hundreds of millions in revenue - while feeling perpetually inadequate. The gap between her external achievements and her internal experience was vast.

The inner critic often masquerades as high standards or realistic self-assessment. But there's a difference between healthy self-evaluation and destructive self-criticism. Healthy evaluation is specific, fair and oriented toward improvement. The inner critic is global, harsh and oriented toward shame.

Alison's silence in that executive meeting wasn't about the specific topic. It was the inner critic running its familiar pattern: *Who are you to speak? They'll see you don't belong here. Better to stay quiet than to be exposed.*

The upgrade: Notice when self-talk becomes self-attack. Ask: "Would I talk to a respected colleague this way?" If not, you're not holding yourself to high standards, you're being cruel to yourself. Alison learned to catch the critic and respond: "That's the old pattern talking. What would I say to someone I respected in this situation?" The reframe didn't silence the critic, but it created space for a different voice.

Which Pattern Costs You Most?

Pause here. Of the patterns we've explored - confirmation bias, attribution error, catastrophizing, availability heuristic, sunk cost fallacy, negativity bias, inner critic - which one creates the most friction in your leadership?

Think about your recent decisions. Which pattern shows up most reliably? Which one has the highest cost when it runs?

Identifying your primary pattern isn't about self-criticism, it's about focus. You can't upgrade all patterns at once. Starting with the one that costs you most creates the highest return on your attention.

Catching Your Patterns in Real Time

The first step to upgrading thought patterns is catching them in operation. This is harder than it sounds because patterns run fast and feel true. The thought "They don't respect me" doesn't feel like a thought, it feels like perception of reality.

Several practices can help:

The pause. When you notice strong emotion or impulse to act, pause. The emotion is a signal that a thought pattern has activated. Before responding, ask: "What thought just ran?"

The journaling practice. This is a more powerful tool than people think and extraordinarily effective for data-driven people. Regular reflection on your thinking reveals patterns that aren't visible in the moment. What situations trigger certain thoughts? What interpretations keep recurring? Jackie started a brief evening practice: three minutes reviewing moments when she'd felt reactive, tracing the thought that preceded the emotion. Within weeks, she could see patterns she'd been blind to for years.

The trusted challenger. Someone who knows you well and will tell you the truth can catch patterns you can't see. David's coach played this role: "You're doing that thing again where you're constructing a case instead of considering the feedback…"

The pattern log. Keep a running record of cognitive patterns you catch. Over time, you'll see which ones are most active and most costly. This data helps prioritize which patterns to work on.

The Upgrade Process

Catching patterns is the first step. Changing them requires deliberate practice:

Step 1: Notice without judgment. The goal isn't to criticize yourself for having cognitive distortions, everyone has them. The goal is to notice them clearly so you can work with them.

Step 2: Label the pattern. "That's confirmation bias" or "That's catastrophizing." Labeling engages your analytical mind and creates distance from the pattern.

Step 3: Generate alternatives. What's another interpretation of this situation? What would a neutral observer see? What would you think if you had different information?

Step 4: Choose deliberately. You may decide your original interpretation was correct. But you've now made a conscious choice rather than an automatic reaction.

Step 5: Track progress. Note when you catch patterns and what you do with them. Celebrate progress while acknowledging that patterns built over decades won't dissolve overnight.

AI as a Thinking Partner

AI can be a powerful tool for working with thought patterns, if you use it deliberately:

Challenge-seeking. Ask AI to challenge your conclusions, find counterevidence, or generate alternative interpretations. "What's wrong with this reasoning?" or "What evidence contradicts this view?"

Perspective-taking. Ask AI to represent different stakeholder perspectives. "How might my team experience this decision?" or "What would a customer say about this approach?"

Red-teaming. Use AI to stress-test your thinking before important decisions. "What could go wrong with this plan?" or "What am I not considering?"

The key is intentional use. If you just ask AI to confirm what you already believe, it will happily do so, confirming your confirmation bias. The leverage comes from using AI deliberately against your cognitive defaults.

From Individual to Collective Patterns

Your thought patterns don't just affect your own leadership, they shape your team's and organization's thinking. Leaders who catastrophize create anxious cultures. Leaders who filter for negative information create environments where problems get attention and progress gets ignored.

Conversely, leaders who model cognitive flexibility - who say "I might be wrong about this" or "What's another interpretation?" - create permission for others to do the same. The upgrade isn't just personal; it's cultural.

Consider how you respond when someone brings you an interpretation that differs from yours. Do you defend your view or get curious about theirs? Do you treat disagreement as threat or as information? Your response in these moments teaches your organization how to think.

The Connection to Behavioral Defaults

Thought patterns don't stay in your head. They drive behavior.

When David's confirmation bias filtered out challenging feedback - he didn't just think differently, he acted differently. He stopped asking genuine questions. He shut down input that contradicted his views. He created the very dynamic his team described in their feedback.

When Sarah catastrophized about AI implementation risks, she didn't just feel anxious - she delayed decisions, demanded more analysis, and created bottlenecks that made some of her fears more likely to materialize.

When Marcus attributed his team's failures to their character, he didn't just judge them internally - he took over their work, denied them growth opportunities, and treated them in ways that confirmed his low expectations.

This is the chain: beliefs shape mindsets, mindsets orient emotional responses, emotions influence thought patterns, and thought patterns drive behavioral defaults. Each component affects the others. But behavioral defaults are where the operating system becomes visible to the outside world.

Your team doesn't see your beliefs, mindsets or thought patterns directly. They see what you do. They experience your behavioral defaults - the automatic actions you take when you don't have time or bandwidth to be deliberate.

That's where we turn next: the behavioral defaults that reveal your operating system to the world, and how to upgrade them so that what people experience matches the leader you intend to be.

BEHAVIORAL DEFAULTS

WHERE YOUR OPERATING SYSTEM MEETS THE WORLD

In Chapter 7, we saw how thought patterns drive behavior. David's confirmation bias led him to stop asking genuine questions. Sarah's catastrophizing caused her to delay decisions. Marcus's attribution errors reinforced his tendency to take over his team's work.

But here's what makes behavioral change so difficult: by the time those thought patterns have run, the behavior has already happened. The action executes faster than conscious awareness. You find yourself doing the thing you swore you wouldn't do, again.

Marcus knew this frustration intimately.

"I know I should delegate more."

He said it with the weariness of someone who had said it many times before. He'd read the leadership books. He'd attended the workshops. He'd received the feedback in three consecutive annual reviews. He understood intellectually that his inability to let go was limiting his team's development and his own advancement.

And yet, here he was again - reviewing work his team had completed, inserting himself into decisions he'd supposedly delegated, unable to resist the gravitational pull of involvement.

"I know what I should do" he told me, frustration evident in his voice. "I just can't seem to actually do it. When the moment comes, something takes over. I'm checking their work before I've consciously decided to look at it."

We've traced Marcus's pattern through this book: the "if I don't do it, who will" belief, the mindset locked in control mode, the emotional processing that made delegation feel viscerally unsafe, the attribution errors that blamed his team's character rather than examining his own contribution.

But understanding all of that hadn't changed what he actually did. When the moment came - when work appeared that he could review, when a decision arose that he could make - his body moved before his mind could intervene. The behavior was automatic.

This is the challenge of behavioral defaults - the automatic responses that execute faster than conscious thought. All the internal work we've explored in previous chapters - beliefs, mindsets, emotional processing, thought patterns - ultimately matters only if it changes what you actually do. And what you actually do is often determined not by deliberate choice but by defaults that run before choice enters the picture.

The Knowing-Doing Gap

Marcus's frustration points to one of the most stubborn realities of leadership development: knowing what to do differently is far easier than actually doing it.

Research consistently shows that information alone rarely changes behavior. Leaders attend training, gain insights, make commitments - and return to their organizations to do exactly what they did before. Not because they're resistant or uncommitted, but because defaults are powerful.

The gap exists because knowledge and behavior operate in different systems. Knowledge lives in your conscious mind, accessible when you have bandwidth to reflect. Behavioral defaults live in automatic processing, executing before reflection can intervene.

When Marcus decided to delegate more, he was making a conscious commitment. When he found himself reviewing his team's work at midnight, a default was running, one that had been reinforced through thousands of repetitions over decades. The conscious commitment was no match for the automatic pattern.

AI-era implication: AI will change what effective leadership behavior looks like - requiring more orchestration, more experimentation, more tolerance for ambiguity. But knowing this won't automatically change your defaults. Leaders who understand AI's implications intellectually may still default to control when AI creates uncertainty. The upgrade requires rewiring the automatic behaviors, not just updating the conscious understanding.

How Defaults Get Built

Your behavioral defaults weren't randomly assigned. They developed through a systematic process of encoding that you largely didn't control.

Reinforcement shapes patterns. Behaviors that produce rewards get repeated. Behaviors that produce pain get avoided. Marcus's control default was built through years of success - he got results by staying close to details, earned promotions by ensuring quality, built his reputation by being the one who could be counted on to fix things. The pattern was reinforced relentlessly until it became automatic.

Stress accelerates encoding. Behaviors performed under stress encode more deeply. The patterns you run when stakes are high become preferentially encoded as your brain learns "this is what to do when it matters." Marcus's control default was forged in the 2008 financial crisis, when his hands-on involvement genuinely saved the firm. That high-stakes success made the pattern nearly unshakeable.

Identity integrates patterns. Over time, defaults become part of how you see yourself. "I'm someone who stays close to the details" or "I'm someone who gets things done." Once a default is integrated into identity, changing it feels like changing who you are.

Contexts trigger patterns. Defaults become associated with specific contexts. A particular meeting room, a certain type of conversation, a familiar kind of pressure - each context can trigger the associated default. Marcus's control default activated in specific contexts: quality reviews, critical decisions, client-facing work. In other contexts, he delegated fine.

The Five Common Leadership Defaults

Through over a decade of coaching executives I've noticed that certain defaults appear with striking regularity among leaders. Recognizing yours is the first step toward upgrading them. We'll explore each through leaders we've come to know.

The Control Default: Marcus's Pattern

Leaders with this default struggle to let go. They review, check, insert themselves, maintain tight oversight. Even when they've consciously decided to delegate, they find themselves pulled back into involvement.

Marcus embodied this default. His calendar was filled with reviews he didn't need to attend. His evenings were spent checking work his team had already completed. His weekends included "just a quick look" at deliverables that were perfectly fine without his input.

The control default often develops in environments where quality genuinely depended on personal involvement, where letting go meant watching things fail. Marcus's version was installed at twelve, reinforced through his early career, and cemented during the crisis when his control actually saved the firm.

The shadow: Control defaults create dependent teams that can't function independently, which confirms the belief that control is necessary, which strengthens the default. Marcus had built exactly what he feared: an organization that couldn't operate without him. The evidence that his team needed oversight was evidence he had created.

AI-era cost: AI implementation requires distributed decision-making at speeds micromanagement can't accommodate. Leaders with unchecked control defaults will become the constraint on AI adoption, unable to let systems operate with appropriate autonomy.

The Expert Default: David's Pattern

Leaders with this default lead with their knowledge - providing answers, demonstrating expertise, being the smartest person in the room. When someone brings a problem, they provide solutions. When someone presents an idea, they evaluate it against their own superior knowledge.

David's 360 feedback revealed this pattern clearly. His questions weren't questions - they were tests to see if people would agree with conclusions he'd already reached. His "input" was actually evaluation. His team had stopped bringing ideas because David always had better ones.

The expert default often develops in careers built on technical excellence. Having answers was the value proposition. Being the expert was the identity. David had spent fifteen years being the one who knew the market - and that expertise had become a trap.

The shadow: Expert defaults shut down others' thinking and development. Teams stop bringing their own solutions because the leader always has better ones. Innovation suffers because ideas have to survive the expert's evaluation before they can be explored.

AI-era cost: AI is the ultimate expert, it can provide answers faster and more comprehensively than any human. Leaders whose value depends on having answers will be displaced. The upgrade is from providing answers to facilitating collective intelligence.

The Accommodation Default: Jackie's Pattern

Leaders with this default say yes when they should say no. They take on too much, agree to unrealistic commitments, struggle to protect boundaries. Their desire to help or to be seen as capable overrides realistic assessment of what's possible.

Remember Jackie in that hospital corridor. Her phone showed seventeen unread messages, her son's call had gone to her assistant, and she was running on four hours of sleep for the third consecutive night. This wasn't an anomaly - it was her accommodation default in action.

Every request felt urgent. Every opportunity seemed essential. Every ask received a yes because saying no felt like failure, like letting people down, like not being the leader everyone needed her to be. She had accommodated her way into exhaustion.

The shadow: Accommodation defaults lead to overcommitment, mediocre delivery on too many fronts, and modeling of unsustainable behavior. The leader burns out while teams learn they can get anything approved regardless of merit.

AI-era cost: AI creates endless new possibilities - tools to evaluate, approaches to consider, implementations to attempt. Leaders who can't say no will be overwhelmed by the optionality. Strategic selection requires protected no.

Two More Defaults to Watch

The Harmony Default. Leaders with this default avoid conflict, smooth over disagreements, prioritize relationship preservation over honest exchange. They tell people what they want to hear rather than what they need to hear. The harmony default often develops in environments where conflict was punishing or where early experiences taught that speaking hard truths led to rejection. *The shadow:* Teams learn not to raise difficult issues because the leader won't engage with them. Unaddressed problems fester until they become crises. *AI-era cost:* AI will displace some roles and change others. Leaders who can't have honest conversations about these changes will leave their teams anxious and uninformed.

The Urgency Default. Leaders with this default treat everything as urgent. They move fast, push for immediate action, struggle to pause and reflect. Speed is their primary mode, regardless of whether speed is actually required. The urgency default often develops in high-pressure environments where fast response was genuinely necessary. *The shadow:* Teams stay in reactive mode, never stepping back to work on the system rather than in it. *AI-era cost:* AI accelerates everything, which can feel like validation for urgency defaults. But AI also creates complexity that requires more reflection, not less. Leaders who can't slow down when needed will make faster and faster mistakes.

Which Default Do You Recognize?

Pause here. Of the five defaults: Control, Expert, Accommodation, Harmony, Urgency - which one shows up most regularly in your leadership?

Think about what you do when pressure rises and you don't have time to be deliberate. Do you grab control? Provide answers? Say yes to everything? Smooth things over? Push for speed?

Most leaders have a primary default and one or two secondary patterns. The primary is the one that runs most automatically, especially under stress. Identifying it is the first step toward choice.

Identifying Your Defaults

Your defaults are often more visible to others than to yourself. By definition, they're automatic, running without the conscious awareness that would make them easy to identify.

Several approaches can help surface your patterns:

Feedback pattern analysis. Review feedback you've received throughout your career. What themes appear repeatedly? The control default shows up as "micromanagement" or "has trouble letting go." The harmony default shows up as "avoids difficult conversations" or "too nice." The patterns in your feedback are data about your defaults.

Stress observation. Notice what you do when pressure increases. Defaults intensify under stress, they're the patterns your brain reaches for when it doesn't have bandwidth for deliberate choice. What happens when you're tired, pressured, or overwhelmed?

Impact inquiry. Ask people who experience your leadership: "What do I do automatically that helps you? What do I do automatically that doesn't help?" Their observations reveal patterns you can't see from inside.

Situation mapping. Identify specific situations where you consistently show up in ways you later regret. What triggers those responses? What pattern is running? Marcus noticed his control default activated specifically around quality-critical work and client-facing deliverables - not everything, but those specific contexts.

What Contexts Trigger Your Default?

Think about the last few times your default ran before you could stop it. What was the context? A particular type of meeting? A certain kind of request? A specific level of stakes?

Defaults don't run uniformly, they're triggered by specific conditions. Identifying your trigger contexts gives you advance warning: when you enter that context, your default is likely to activate. That awareness creates a small but crucial gap for choice.

The Upgrade Process

Behavioral defaults won't change through insight alone. They require systematic intervention that builds new patterns strong enough to compete with the old ones.

1. Awareness Before Choice

The first step is developing awareness of the default in real time - not after the fact, but in the moment. This requires building a trigger awareness practice.

Identify the contexts, emotions, and situations that typically activate your default. For Marcus, it was seeing work his team had completed, especially anything client-facing. For Jackie, it was receiving any request framed as urgent or important. For David, it was hearing an idea that differed from his own analysis.

Practice noticing these triggers as they occur. Not judging, not yet trying to change anything - just noticing. "Ah, this is the situation where my control default usually activates." This awareness creates the gap between trigger and response where choice becomes possible.

2. Alternative Behavior Installation

Decide specifically what you want to do instead. Not a vague intention to "be different" but a concrete alternative behavior you can execute.

For Marcus's control default: "When I feel the urge to review, I will ask: Is my involvement necessary for this decision? If not, I will ask a question rather than provide direction."

For Jackie's accommodation default: "When I receive a request, I will say 'Let me check my priorities and get back to you' rather than answering immediately. I will evaluate against my strategic priorities before committing."

For David's expert default: "When someone presents an idea, I will ask three questions before offering my perspective. I will be curious before I am evaluative."

The alternative behavior needs to be specific enough to execute in the moment, when you don't have bandwidth for complex deliberation.

3. Repetition Under Progressive Challenge

New behaviors become defaults through repetition. Start with lower-stakes situations where the old default is less intense. Build confidence and neural pathway strength. Then progressively increase the challenge.

Marcus began by stepping back from low-stakes internal reviews. As that became comfortable, he tackled medium-stakes decisions. Eventually, he built the capacity to step back from high-stakes client work that would have been impossible earlier. The progression took months, not weeks.

4. Environmental Support

Design your environment to support new behaviors and interrupt old defaults.

Marcus removed himself from certain review meetings, not because he couldn't attend, but because removing the opportunity interrupted the automatic default. Jackie blocked "decision time" in her calendar - protected space where she evaluated requests against priorities rather than responding in the moment. David asked his team to present ideas without his presence first, so they could develop their thinking before his expert default could shut it down.

5. Stakeholder Involvement

Involving others in behavior change dramatically increases success rates. Select stakeholders who will observe your behavior in action. Tell them what you're working on. Ask for ongoing feedforward— suggestions for how you might improve in the future. Follow up monthly to check progress.

This approach builds accountability (you're more likely to change when others are watching), provides data (they see patterns you can't), and demonstrates commitment (which itself builds trust and permission for the new behavior).

Marcus told his direct reports what he was working on: "I'm practicing stepping back. When you see me starting to take over, I'm asking you to tell me. And when I do step back successfully, I'd appreciate knowing that too." The transparency itself changed the dynamic, his team became partners in his development rather than observers of his default.

Working with Setbacks

Defaults don't disappear when you adopt alternatives - they remain available, ready to reassert themselves when conditions favor them. Setbacks are inevitable.

The question isn't whether you'll revert to old defaults, you will. The question is how you respond to that reversion.

Treat setbacks as data, not failure. What triggered the reversion? What conditions were present? What can you learn about the circumstances that activate your default? Each setback reveals something useful.

Resume practice quickly. The longer you stay in the old pattern, the stronger it becomes relative to the new one. Notice the reversion, understand it, and get back to practicing the alternative.

Adjust strategies. If setbacks occur in similar circumstances, that's information about where your current approach isn't working. Perhaps you need additional support in those specific contexts, or perhaps the alternative behavior needs refinement.

The Leadership You Practice

Your leadership isn't defined by what you know about leadership. It's defined by what you do. The sophisticated frameworks in your head matter far less than the behaviors your team experiences. The elegant theories you espouse mean nothing compared to the actions you take when pressure rises.

Marcus eventually changed. Not through another workshop or a deeper insight, but through sustained practice of different behaviors in the situations that had triggered his old defaults. The control default didn't disappear, but a new pattern of delegation became strong enough to compete with it.

He still has to practice. The old default is still there, ready to reassert itself when conditions favor it. But he's no longer a prisoner of patterns formed decades ago. He has choice.

"The belief is still there," he told me in one of our final coaching sessions. "When something important is happening, I still feel the pull to be involved. But now I can notice the pull without acting on it. I can ask myself: Is this about the work, or is this about my anxiety? Usually, it's about my anxiety. And I've learned that I can tolerate the anxiety without letting it run my behavior."

That's the upgrade: not eliminating the default, but building enough capacity around it to choose.

The Question of Direction

Here's what Marcus discovered as his behavioral defaults came under his control: having choice about how to behave raised a deeper question. If he wasn't going to run his old patterns automatically, what would guide his choices instead?

The answer couldn't be more sophisticated analysis of each situation, that would be too slow and too exhausting. He needed something else. A compass. A set of principles that could guide behavior when deliberation wasn't possible.

He needed clarity on his values.

Values are the sixth component of your leadership operating system - the compass that determines direction. Without clarity on values, all the upgrades we've developed - beliefs, mindsets, emotional processing, thought patterns, behaviors - lack coherent direction. You might be running an optimized system toward a destination you never actually wanted to reach.

That's where we turn next.

⬥

VALUES ALIGNMENT

YOUR INNER COMPASS FOR LEADERSHIP DECISIONS

In Chapter 8, Marcus discovered something unexpected. As his behavioral defaults came under his control, as he built the capacity to choose rather than react, a deeper question emerged: If he wasn't going to run his old patterns automatically, what would guide his choices instead?

He couldn't deliberate every decision from scratch. That would be too slow and too exhausting. He needed something else. A compass. A set of principles that could guide behavior when deliberation wasn't possible.

He needed clarity on his values.

But values aren't just about guiding moment-to-moment choices. They're about something more fundamental: whether the life you're building is actually the life you want. Whether the success you're pursuing will satisfy you when you achieve it. Whether you're climbing a mountain you actually want to summit.

Jackie understood this question intimately, though it took her years to name it.

The Hollow Achievement

Remember Jackie in that hospital corridor? The COO who had built her career on being the one who could handle anything, who never dropped a ball, who was always available?

By every external measure, she was successful. She'd achieved the title, the compensation, the scope of responsibility. She led a major healthcare organization through a period of unprecedented change. She was respected, sought-after, admired.

And she was exhausted in a way that sleep couldn't fix.

"I'm doing everything right," she told me in one of our early sessions. "I'm hitting my numbers. I'm advancing the mission. But something feels hollow. I keep asking myself: Is this it? Is this what I worked so hard for?"

When we explored deeper, a pattern emerged. Jackie had optimized for achievement without clarifying what she actually valued. She'd climbed efficiently without asking whether she was climbing the right mountain. The goals she'd pursued were impressive but disconnected from what genuinely mattered to her.

Her son's calls going to her assistant. Her weekends consumed by work she couldn't remember choosing. Her identity so merged with her role that she couldn't distinguish between what the organization needed and what she needed. These weren't just symptoms of over-work, they were symptoms of values misalignment.

This is values misalignment - the gap between how you're spending your leadership energy and what you actually care about. It produces a particular kind of suffering: the suffering of success that doesn't satisfy, of achievement that doesn't fulfill, of winning games you never consciously chose to play.

Values are the sixth component of your leadership operating system. They're the compass that determines direction - not what you want to achieve, but who you want to be and how you want to lead. Without clarity on values, all the other components we've developed - beliefs, mindsets, emotional processing, thought patterns, behaviors - lack coherent direction. You might be running an optimized system toward a destination you never actually wanted to reach.

What Values Actually Are

Values are personally chosen life directions. They're your inner compass - not about what you want to get or achieve, but about how you want to behave on an ongoing basis, how you want to treat yourself, others, and the world around you.

This definition matters because it distinguishes values from several things they're often confused with.

Values Are Not Goals

Goals are things you can achieve, check off, complete. You can reach a goal and be done with it. Values are directions you move in continuously - they're never finished, never fully achieved.

"Become CEO" was a goal Jackie achieved. "Lead with integrity" is a value she could embody more fully every day for the rest of her career. You can achieve a promotion and then wonder what's next. You can never fully achieve integrity - you can only keep moving in that direction, embodying it more fully in each decision.

Goals are places you arrive. Values are how you travel. Jackie had achieved her goals, and discovered that goals without underlying values leave you successful but adrift.

Values Are Not Feelings

You might not feel courageous in a given moment, but you can still behave courageously. You might not feel compassionate when someone has frustrated you, but you can still act with compassion. Values describe how you want to act, not how you want to feel.

This distinction is crucial because it means values remain accessible even when emotions are difficult. You can honor your value of honesty even when you feel afraid of the reaction. Values provide guidance precisely when feelings would lead you astray.

Values Are Chosen, Not Imposed

Values are qualities we choose freely. As soon as we start to feel we have to follow a value, it loses all its vitality. It stops being a value and starts being a rule.

Many leaders carry values that aren't actually theirs - values inherited from parents, absorbed from organizational culture, adopted to meet others' expectations. These borrowed values might look good on paper, but they don't provide genuine guidance because they don't connect to what the leader actually cares about.

Jackie had absorbed a value of "availability" from her organizational culture - the belief that leaders should always be accessible, always responsive, always on. It looked like dedication, but it wasn't a value she had consciously chosen. It was an expectation she had internalized. And it was draining her.

Authentic values feel vitalizing, not obligating. They generate energy rather than drain it. When you're living according to your genuine values, even difficult work feels meaningful. When you're living according to imposed values, even success feels hollow.

What Do You Actually Value?

Pause here. Before reading further, consider: What do you actually value in your leadership?

Not what you think you should value. Not what your organization rewards. Not what sounds impressive. What genuinely matters to you about how you lead?

If you're not sure, notice what bothers you. Values violations create friction. When something feels wrong in your leadership—even if you can't articulate why—there's often a value being violated. What patterns of discomfort might reveal values you haven't named?

The Values Yardstick

How do you know if something is truly a value for you? Ask: Does it bring vitality and meaning to my life - even when things are hard or stressful?

Genuine values sustain you through difficulty. They dignify the normal pain that comes with living and provide motivation even when things are hard. If something only matters to you when it's easy, it's probably a preference, not a value.

A leader who genuinely values innovation will persist through the frustration of failed experiments. A leader who values development will invest in difficult feedback conversations even when they're uncomfortable. A leader who values integrity will tell hard truths even when silence would be easier. The value carries them through the difficulty rather than evaporating when difficulty arrives.

Why Values Matter for Leadership

With all the demands of leadership, it's easy to lose sight of what's important. Your actions can be driven by immediate pressures, organizational expectations, or old habits rather than by conscious choice about what matters. Values serve as a guide when the path isn't clear.

Values as Decision Filters

Leaders face countless decisions, many more than they can analyze deeply. Values provide filtering criteria that enable faster, more consistent decisions. When you're clear that you value transparency, the decision about whether to share difficult information becomes simpler. When you're clear that you value development, the decision about whether to invest time in coaching becomes obvious.

Without clear values, every decision requires fresh deliberation. With clear values, many decisions become straightforward applications of principles you've already established.

AI-era application: AI will present you with more decisions, more options, more information than you can possibly process deliberatively. Your values become the filter that enables you to move through this complexity without being paralyzed by it. Without that filter, AI's optionality becomes overwhelming.

Values as Consistency Anchors

Leadership impact depends on consistency. Teams learn to predict your behavior, trust your commitments, and rely on your judgment only when you show up consistently over time. Values provide the anchor for that consistency.

A leader whose actions seem random or unpredictable undermines trust, even if individual decisions are reasonable. A leader whose actions clearly flow from stable values builds trust, even when specific decisions are controversial. People may disagree with the decision while still respecting that it's consistent with who you are.

Values as Energy Sources

Values-aligned leadership generates energy rather than depleting it. When your work connects to what you genuinely care about, even demanding effort feels sustainable. When your work conflicts with your values, even moderate effort feels draining.

Jackie was working hard - but against herself. Her success demanded behaviors that conflicted with values she'd never articulated but still held. The misalignment created a constant friction that drained her regardless of how much she achieved.

Discovering Your Values

If you've been running on autopilot, pursuing goals and meeting expectations without reflection, you may need to actively discover what you actually value.

The Life Review

Reflect on moments when you felt most alive, most yourself, most satisfied - not because of external achievement but because of internal alignment. What values were you expressing in those moments?

Equally instructive are moments of violation - times when something felt deeply wrong, when you acted against something that mattered and felt the cost. What values were being violated?

When Jackie did this exercise, she discovered something surprising. The moments she felt most alive weren't her biggest achievements - the promotions, the successful initiatives, the industry recognition. They were moments of genuine connection: a conversation where she helped someone see themselves differently, a team coming together around a shared purpose, her son asking her opinion about something that mattered to him.

Her moments of greatest violation weren't failures, she could handle failure. They were moments when she'd sacrificed connection for achievement: missing her son's events for meetings that could have been rescheduled, choosing efficiency over presence, optimizing for outcomes at the cost of relationships.

The pattern was clear, once she looked: connection was a core value she'd been systematically violating in pursuit of goals that didn't actually require the sacrifice.

The Values Inventory

Consider values across different domains:

How do you want to treat yourself? How do you want to treat others? How do you want to show up in your work? How do you want to engage with challenges and growth? How do you want to contribute to the broader world?

Don't list what sounds good, list what's actually true for you. A value you feel you should have but don't genuinely hold is not a value. It's an expectation you've absorbed.

The Priority Test

If you generate a long list of values, you haven't yet done the differentiation work. Everything can't be equally important. When values conflict, as they will, which ones take priority?

Imagine scenarios where values conflict: Transparency conflicts with kindness when the truth is painful. Achievement conflicts with well-being when success requires unsustainable effort. Loyalty conflicts with integrity when the team is heading in the wrong direction.

How you resolve these conflicts reveals your actual value hierarchy, not what you say is important, but what actually drives decisions when trade-offs are required.

THE ALIGNMENT ASSESSMENT

This is the work I do with my clients in our coaching sessions - and it's where the real gaps become undeniable.

Once you've clarified your values, the question becomes: How aligned is your actual leadership with those values?

Return to your calendar. You did this diagnostic work in Chapter 3. Look at it again through the lens of your clarified values. Jackie's calendar audit was devastating: less than two percent of her time was spent on the connection she'd identified as a core value. What does yours reveal?

Decision review. Consider the significant decisions you've made recently. What values did they actually reflect? Not what you told yourself, but what an observer would infer from your choices.

Impact inquiry. Ask people who experience your leadership what they think you value, based purely on your behavior. Their observations reveal your operating values - which may differ from your espoused values.

Gaps between espoused values and operating values aren't hypocrisy - they're the clearest indicator of where your operating system needs attention. Every gap represents a place where something is overriding your conscious intentions. And closing those gaps is rarely something leaders can do alone.

Where Are Your Gaps?

Consider your own values alignment. If you examined your calendar, your decisions, and asked people who work with you - what would the gaps reveal?

Where are you spending energy on things that don't connect to what you actually value? Where are you sacrificing what matters for what's merely urgent? Where has your operating system drifted from your conscious intentions?

These gaps aren't failures, they're information. They show you where the upgrade work is most needed.

AI-Era Values Challenges

AI creates specific values challenges that deserve attention:

Efficiency versus Humanity. AI enables extraordinary efficiency, but efficiency isn't a value, it's a means. What are you being efficient in service of? Leaders who optimize for AI efficiency without values clarity may find they've optimized away things that mattered.

Speed versus Wisdom. AI accelerates everything, including decisions. But wisdom often requires deliberateness: reflection, consideration, perspective. How do you preserve the values that require patience in an environment that rewards speed?

Scale versus Connection. AI enables scale that was previously impossible. But scale can dilute the human connection that many leaders value. Jackie faced this directly: AI could help her organization serve more patients, but would it preserve the quality of care she valued?

Innovation versus stability. AI rewards constant innovation. But some values - community, tradition, stability - are served by continuity rather than change. How do you honor both innovation and the values that thrive in stability?

Closing the Gap

Values alignment isn't achieved once and maintained automatically. It requires ongoing attention, noticing gaps as they emerge and making adjustments to close them.

Structural changes. Some misalignments require structural solutions. If you value development but never have time for it, the answer might be changing your calendar structure rather than trying harder. If you value innovation but your role is entirely operational, the answer might be changing the role.

Boundary setting. Some misalignments require saying no. If you value sustainability but keep accommodating requests that create unsustainable load, the answer is better boundaries. This often means disappointing others in service of values, which requires clarity about what matters more.

Values conversations. Some misalignments require explicit negotiation. If organizational demands conflict with personal values, the conversation might be with stakeholders about what trade-offs are acceptable. If team expectations conflict with values, the conversation might be about different ways of working.

Jackie's Realignment

Jackie's values work didn't produce a dramatic career change. She didn't quit her job or abandon her ambitions. But it fundamentally restructured how she approached her leadership.

She identified three core values that had been running beneath her awareness: connection, integrity and growth. Not growth as achievement - growth as development, learning, becoming. These values had been present all along, but she'd been systematically sacrificing them for goals that didn't actually require the sacrifice.

The structural changes came first. She blocked time for one-on-one conversations that weren't about operational issues, time to actually connect with her team as people. She protected her weekends not as rest from work but as time for connection with her family. She restructured her AI implementation approach to preserve the human touchpoints she valued in patient care.

The boundary setting came harder. She had to disappoint people who expected her constant availability. She had to say no to opportunities that would have advanced her career but violated her values. She had to tolerate the discomfort of being less than everything to everyone.

"The hardest part wasn't knowing what I valued," she told me. "It was accepting that I couldn't have everything. That choosing connection meant not choosing some achievements. That honoring my values meant disappointing some expectations."

The external metrics didn't change dramatically, she remained successful by conventional measures. But the internal experience transformed. Success that had felt hollow began to feel meaningful. Achievement that had drained her began to energize her. The corridor that night became a memory of who she used to be, not a prediction of who she would remain.

"I'm still ambitious," she said in one of our final sessions. "I still want to achieve. But now I know what the achievement is for. It's in service of values I've consciously chosen, not goals I absorbed without examination. That makes all the difference."

From Values to Expression

Here's what Jackie discovered as her values became clear: knowing your values isn't enough. You have to express them. You have to communicate them. You have to make them visible to the people you lead.

Values that stay inside your head don't shape relationships. They don't build culture. They don't create the alignment that transforms individual leadership into collective movement. For values to have impact beyond your own choices, they have to become part of how you communicate.

And communication isn't just what you say - it's how you say it, when you say it, what you don't say, and whether your words match your actions. It's the seventh and final component of your leadership operating system: the protocols that determine how your internal architecture shows up in relationships.

That's where we turn next.

❧

CHAPTER TEN

COMMUNICATION PROTOCOLS

WHERE YOUR OPERATING SYSTEM CONNECTS WITH OTHERS

In Chapter 9, Jackie discovered that values clarified in private mean nothing until they're expressed in public. Her value of connection had to become visible in how she showed up - in conversations, decisions and relationships. Values that stay inside your head don't shape culture or build trust.

This is true for every component of your operating system. Your upgraded beliefs, mindsets, emotional processing, thought patterns, behavioral defaults, and values all exist inside you. But leadership happens between you and others. The only way your internal operating system reaches the people you lead is through communication.

Communication is the interface layer, where everything we've explored in Part Two meets the external world. And like any interface, it can transmit cleanly or create distortion. It can build connection or generate distance. It can amplify your leadership effectiveness or undermine it, regardless of how well the rest of your system is functioning.

David learned this the hard way.

The Message That Didn't Land

Six months after receiving his 360-degree feedback, David thought he'd made real progress. He'd processed the emotional devastation of discovering his self-perception was wrong. He'd examined his thought patterns, the confirmation bias, the attribution errors. He'd begun practicing curiosity instead of certainty.

But something still wasn't working.

He'd just finished what he thought was a developmental feedback conversation with one of his best engineers. He'd been specific about what needed to improve. He'd provided concrete examples. He'd even mentioned several things that were going well. He'd worked hard to approach it with curiosity rather than his old certainty.

And now she was in tears, convinced she was about to be fired.

"I thought I was being helpful," he told me, genuinely confused. "I said exactly what the training taught me to say. I even started with something positive. I was trying to be curious, not certain. How did it go so wrong?"

This is the puzzle of communication: the meaning you send is often not the meaning that lands. You intend to develop; they feel criticized. You intend to empower; they feel micromanaged. You intend to be clear; they feel dismissed. The words are the same, but the meaning that lands is entirely different from the meaning you sent.

David had upgraded his internal operating system. But his communication protocols, the patterns through which that system expressed itself, were still running old code. His words said curiosity, but his delivery, his framing, his history with this person, all transmitted something else entirely.

The Intent-Impact Gap

David's situation illustrates a fundamental truth about communication: you don't get credit for your intent. You only get the results of your impact.

Intent lives inside you - it's what you mean, what you're trying to accomplish, what you hope the other person will experience. Impact lives outside you - it's what actually lands, how the other person actually experiences your communication.

The gap between intent and impact exists because communication isn't transmission, it's construction. You don't send meaning directly into another person's mind. You send signals - words, tone, facial expressions, timing, context - and the other person constructs meaning from those signals using their own operating system.

David intended development. But his engineer's operating system - shaped by past experiences with his critical feedback style, beliefs about what detailed criticism means, and emotional patterns around evaluation by authority figures - constructed a different meaning. Same signals, different construction, completely different experience.

Why Intent Doesn't Equal Impact

Context shapes interpretation. The same words mean different things in different contexts. "We need to talk" from a peer suggests collaboration. The same words from a boss with a history of critical feedback trigger anxiety.

History creates filters. Every interaction is interpreted through the lens of previous interactions. David's engineer had experienced years of his expert default, questions that weren't questions, input that was really evaluation. Even when his intent changed, her filters were calibrated to his old pattern.

Emotional states distort reception. A person in a calm state processes communication differently than a person who's stressed or anxious. David's engineer was already feeling uncertain about a project that hadn't gone well. The feedback arrived into a system primed for threat detection.

Power dynamics amplify everything. Communication from leaders carries more weight than the same communication from peers. A mild concern expressed by David became serious criticism when filtered through the power dynamics between VP and engineer.

Taking Responsibility for Impact

The intent-impact gap creates a choice: you can insist on being judged by your intent, or you can take responsibility for your impact.

Leaders who insist on intent defend themselves when communication goes wrong: "That's not what I meant." "You misunderstood me." "I was trying to help." These statements may be true, but they don't change the impact. They shift the problem to the receiver and leave the damage unrepaired.

Leaders who take responsibility for impact approach things differently. They recognize that impact is the only thing that matters because impact is the only thing that exists outside their own head. When impact diverges from intent, they get curious: What happened? How was this received? What did I miss?

AI-era implication: AI-mediated communication - automated messages, AI-generated content, AI-facilitated decisions - creates new intent-impact gaps. The leader's intent gets filtered through AI before reaching the recipient. Understanding how AI affects communication impact becomes a critical skill.

Communication Defaults

Just as you have behavioral defaults, you have communication defaults - habitual patterns for how you share information, receive input and navigate conflict.

Sharing Defaults

How do you default when sharing information? Some leaders default to comprehensiveness, extensive context, multiple considerations. Others default to brevity, bottom-line first, minimal context. Some default to certainty, conclusions as settled. Others default to provisionality, hedging, qualifying.

David's sharing default had been certainty. When he shared a perspective, it came across as settled, final, not open for discussion. Even when he was genuinely uncertain, his delivery conveyed authority that shut down dialogue. His words might say "What do you think?" but his tone said, "Here's the answer."

Receiving Defaults

How do you default when receiving input? Some leaders default to evaluation - immediately assessing right or wrong. Others default to inquiry - exploring before judging. Some default to defense - explaining, justifying. Others default to absorption - taking in without visible reaction.

David's receiving default had been evaluation. When someone presented an idea, his mind immediately went to assessment mode: Is this right? What's wrong with it? How does it compare to what I would have done? His 360 feedback had named this precisely: his questions weren't questions, they were tests.

Receiving defaults shape what information reaches you. If people know you default to evaluation, they soften their input or withhold it entirely. David had inadvertently trained his team to stop bringing ideas because the evaluation process was too punishing.

Conflict Defaults

How do you default when conflict arises? Some default to avoidance - smoothing, minimizing tension. Others default to confrontation - engaging directly. Some default to accommodation - yielding to preserve relationship. Others default to competition - advocating strongly for their position.

Conflict defaults often trace to early experiences. Leaders who grew up in families where conflict was destructive often develop avoidance defaults. Those who learned that conflict was how issues got resolved often develop confrontation defaults.

What Are Your Communication Defaults?

Pause here. Consider your own patterns:

When you share information, do you default to comprehensive or brief? Certain or provisional? What does your delivery communicate beyond your words?

When you receive input, do you default to evaluation or inquiry? Defense or absorption? What does your receiving pattern teach people about what they can bring you?

When conflict arises, do you default to avoidance or confrontation?

Accommodation or competition? What does your conflict pattern create over time?

Your defaults are visible to others even when they're invisible to you. The patterns you can't see are shaping every interaction.

CLEAR PACE™: A Communication Upgrade Framework

Effective communication in complex environments requires moving beyond defaults to conscious choice. CLEAR PACE™ provides a framework for upgrading communication protocols.

When David and I examined his failed feedback conversation, we used this framework to understand what had gone wrong, and what could be different.

CLEAR: The Foundation

C - Context. Set the frame before delivering the content. What's the purpose of this communication? What should the listener be focusing on?

David had jumped straight to feedback without establishing that his intent was development, not evaluation. His engineer's operating system, calibrated to years of David's evaluative pattern, filled in the missing context with threat: *He's about to criticize my work.*

L - Listen first. Before delivering your message, understand where the other person is starting from. What's their current state? What context are they bringing?

David hadn't asked how his engineer was feeling before diving into specifics. Had he checked, he would have learned she was already anxious about the project, and could have adjusted his approach accordingly.

E - Empathize. Demonstrate that you understand their perspective, even if you disagree with it. Make them feel seen before you try to be heard.

David had skipped this entirely. He was so focused on delivering his message that he never acknowledged the pressure she was under or the effort she'd already invested. She felt evaluated, not understood.

A - Articulate clearly. Say what you mean directly, without excessive softening or unnecessary harshness. Clarity serves people; confusion doesn't.

Ironically, David thought he was being clear. But clarity isn't just about your words - it's about what lands. His message ("I want to help you grow") got lost in his delivery ("Here's what you're doing wrong").

R - Request response. Check what was received. "What are you hearing?" or "What questions does this raise?" Close the loop to verify intent matched impact.

This was David's biggest miss. He'd delivered his message without checking what landed. Had he asked "What are you taking away from this?" he could have corrected the misinterpretation before tears appeared.

PACE: The Delivery

P - Presence. Full attention, not distracted or hurried. People sense when you're not fully present, and it affects how they receive your communication.

David had scheduled the conversation between two other meetings. His engineer could feel his time pressure, which signaled: *This isn't important enough for his full attention - or I'm not.*

A - Authenticity. Speak from your genuine perspective rather than performing a leadership persona. Authentic communication builds trust; performed communication triggers suspicion.

David realized he'd been performing "developmental leader" rather than being genuinely present. His engineer sensed the performance, and it undermined trust in his message.

C - Calibration. Adjust your communication to the person and context. What works with one team member may not work with another. What's appropriate in one situation may be wrong in another.

David used the same direct approach with everyone. But this engineer needed more warmth and reassurance than others on his team. His failure to calibrate turned useful feedback into a painful experience.

E - Emotional awareness. Monitor both your emotional state and theirs. When emotions escalate, communication effectiveness decreases. Sometimes the best communication move is to pause and let emotions settle.

When David saw tears forming, he pushed forward - trying to "fix" the conversation by explaining his intent. What his engineer needed was a pause, not more words.

High-Stakes Communication

The stakes of communication amplify everything, both potential impact and potential for damage. High-stakes conversations require additional attention.

Preparation matters more. In low-stakes communication, you can recover from missteps easily. In high-stakes communication, the cost of getting it wrong is significant. What's your intent? What impact do you want to create? What might they be feeling coming into this conversation? What history is relevant?

Emotional regulation is critical. High stakes activate threat responses. When your nervous system is activated, communication quality degrades. The practices from Chapter 6 - physiological reset, naming intervention, perspective shift - are essential preparation for high-stakes conversations.

Recovery protocols are essential. Despite best efforts, high-stakes communications sometimes go wrong. When you realize impact isn't matching intent: "I'm noticing this isn't landing the way I intended. Can we pause and reset?" When emotions escalate: "I think we'd both benefit from some time to process before we continue." When you've clearly made an error: "I got that wrong. Let me try again."

Where Do You Need to Practice?

Consider the CLEAR PACE ™ elements. Where are your gaps?

Do you set context, or jump straight to content? Do you listen first, or deliver first? Do you check what message was received, or assume it matched what you sent?

Are you fully present, or often distracted? Authentic, or performing? Calibrated to the person, or one-size-fits-all? Aware of emotions, or blindsided by them?

Choose one element to focus on. Practice in low-stakes situations until it becomes more natural. Then extend to higher-stakes contexts. Communication protocols upgrade through practice, not understanding.

AI-Era Communication

AI changes communication in ways leaders must understand:

AI-mediated messages. Increasingly, communication happens through AI-assisted tools - email suggestions, automated summaries, AI-generated reports. Leaders must understand how AI affects the signals that reach recipients and be deliberate about when human-direct communication is essential.

Communicating about AI. How you communicate about AI - with enthusiasm or anxiety, clarity or confusion—shapes how your organization experiences AI transformation. Your communication about AI is leadership of the transformation.

Human communication as differentiator. As AI handles more transactional communication, human communication must handle what AI can't - the emotional, relational, adaptive work that requires genuine human presence. The bar for human communication rises.

Speed and reflection. AI enables faster communication cycles, but not all communication benefits from speed. Leaders must discern when AI-enabled speed serves communication and when it undermines the reflection that important messages require.

David's Communication Upgrade

David practiced deliberately. He started with low-stakes conversations, consciously working through CLEAR PACE ™ before each one. It felt awkward at first, mechanical, forced. But the awkwardness was the feeling of building new neural pathways.

Context became his anchor. Before any significant conversation, he would explicitly name the purpose: "I want to explore something with you", "I'm genuinely curious about your perspective" or "I have some feedback that I think will help you grow." The framing alone changed how people received what followed.

Listening first was harder. His expert default wanted to jump to his perspective, his evaluation, his answer. He had to physically slow himself down, asking questions and genuinely attending to the answers before sharing his view.

Requesting response became his most valuable tool. "What are you hearing?" or "Tell me what you're taking away from this" gave him real-time data about the intent-impact gap. He caught misinterpretations before they calcified into beliefs.

Three months after the failed feedback conversation, David had another developmental discussion with the same engineer. Same type of content: areas for growth, specific observations, developmental suggestions.

This time, he started differently: "I'd like to share some observations that I think could help you take on more complex projects. This isn't about anything being wrong, it's about what would help you grow. Does this feel like a good time to discuss this?"

She said yes. He listened to how she was experiencing her current work before sharing his perspective. He checked what she was hearing throughout. At the end, he asked: "What's your main takeaway from this conversation?"

"That you see potential in me," she said. "And that you're invested in helping me develop it."

Same developmental intent. Same type of content. Completely different impact, because the communication protocols had been upgraded.

The Complete Operating System

Your communication is how your leadership reaches the world. All the internal work we've explored - beliefs, mindsets, emotions, thoughts, behaviors, values - expresses through this interface. Upgrading your communication protocols is how you ensure that the upgraded operating system actually produces upgraded outcomes.

With this chapter, we've completed the seven components of your leadership operating system:

Belief Architecture - the foundational assumptions that shape what you see as possible

Mindsets - the orientations that determine how you approach challenges

Emotional Processing - the capacity that determines how you lead under pressure

Thought Patterns - the cognitive habits that shape your interpretation of reality

Behavioral Defaults - the automatic actions that reveal your operating system to the world

Values Alignment - the compass that provides direction for all the other components

Communication Protocols - the interface through which your leadership connects with others

Each component affects the others. Beliefs shape mindsets. Mindsets influence emotional responses. Emotions affect thought patterns. Thought patterns drive behavioral defaults. Values provide direction. And communication is how the whole system expresses itself in relationships.

We've explored each component separately to understand it clearly. But in lived leadership, they don't operate separately. They operate as a system - interdependent, mutually reinforcing, constantly interacting.

In Part Three, we turn from the components themselves to what emerges when they work together. An upgraded operating system doesn't just function better - it produces new capabilities. The five premium skillsets of AI-era leadership aren't things you bolt on; they're what naturally arise when your internal architecture is aligned and optimized.

The leaders we've followed - Jackie, Marcus, David, Sarah, Alison - didn't just upgrade individual components. Their real breakthroughs came when upgraded components began working together, producing capabilities they couldn't have developed any other way.

That's where we go next.

❧

END OF PART TWO

PART THREE

FROM INSIGHT TO INTEGRATION

THE FIVE EMERGING SKILLSETS

THE CAPABILITIES THAT ARISE WHEN YOUR OPERATING SYSTEM INTEGRATES

The paradox hit Jackie in her third year as COO.

She had spent two decades building the capabilities that got her to the top - operational excellence, clinical knowledge, relentless execution. Every promotion had validated these strengths. Every success had reinforced them.

Now, leading a healthcare system through major transformation, she realized something unsettling: the capabilities that got her here wouldn't keep her here. The very strengths that had driven her ascent were becoming obstacles to her effectiveness at this level.

"I was still trying to be the best individual performer," she told me later. "But the job wasn't about my performance anymore. It was about everyone else's. And I didn't have the skills for that."

This is the emerging skillset gap. The seven operating system components we explored in Part Two - beliefs, mindsets, emotional processing, thought patterns, behavioral defaults, values, and communication - are necessary but not sufficient for exceptional leadership. They're the foundation. On that foundation, specific capabilities emerge that translate internal architecture into external impact.

These are the five emerging skillsets: Cognitive Flexibility, Emotional Intelligence at Scale, Human-AI Collaboration Design, Strategic Sensemaking and Exponential Thinking. Unlike skills you can develop through training programs, these capabilities emerge when your seven operating system components are upgraded and working together. They're the second layer of the 7-5-3 Human Upgrade Code™ - what arises naturally when the foundation is solid.

Why Emerging Skillsets Matter Now

Every leader has some level of capability in these domains. You don't reach senior positions without being able to think flexibly, read emotional dynamics, work with technology, make sense of complexity and adapt to change. The question isn't whether you have these skills, it's whether you've developed them to the level your current challenges require.

What counted as adequate ten years ago no longer suffices. The complexity of decisions has increased. The speed of required adaptation has accelerated. The emotional demands on leaders have intensified. The need to work effectively with AI has become non-negotiable.

And here's the crucial insight: you can't develop these skillsets directly through training. They emerge from the integration of your operating system components. This chapter explains what each skillset looks like at mastery level and how it arises from the foundational work you've done.

Skillset One: Cognitive Flexibility

Cognitive flexibility is the capacity to switch between mental frameworks, hold multiple perspectives simultaneously, question your own assumptions, and adapt your thinking in real-time as new information emerges.

Leaders with high cognitive flexibility can entertain contradictory ideas without anxiety. They can argue passionately for a position and then genuinely consider its opposite. They don't confuse changing their mind with weakness, they see it as intelligence responding to reality.

How It Emerges

This skillset emerges from the integration of upgraded beliefs (Chapter 4) and mindsets (Chapter 5). When you've done the work of examining your foundational assumptions and developing the five mindset upgrades, cognitive flexibility becomes available.

The connection is direct: rigid beliefs produce rigid thinking. If your belief architecture treats your assumptions as facts rather than hypotheses, you can't flex. If your mindset demands certainty, you'll resist information that creates uncertainty. But when beliefs become genuinely examinable and curiosity replaces the need for certainty, cognitive flexibility emerges as a natural byproduct.

Signs of Mastery

- You can articulate the strongest case against your own position
- You regularly update your views based on new evidence

- You can hold strategic direction while remaining genuinely open to pivoting

- You find contradictory information interesting rather than threatening

Skillset Two: Emotional Intelligence at Scale

Emotional intelligence at scale extends individual EQ to collective emotional dynamics - reading, responding to, and shaping the emotional landscape of teams, organizations, and stakeholder ecosystems.

How It Emerges

This skillset emerges from upgraded emotional processing (Chapter 6) combined with communication protocols (Chapter 10). When you can regulate your own emotions under pressure AND communicate in ways that create psychological safety, you gain the ability to manage collective emotional states.

The sequence matters. You can't regulate others if you can't regulate yourself. You can't create safety if your own anxiety is contagious. But when your emotional processing is upgraded - when you can stay present with difficult emotions without being hijacked - your capacity extends outward. You become someone who calms rooms rather than escalates them.

Signs of Mastery

- You can read the emotional state of a room within minutes of entering

- You notice when collective anxiety is rising before it becomes crisis

- Your presence tends to calm rather than escalate tense situations

- You can hold space for collective grief, fear, or uncertainty without rushing to fix it

Skillset Three: Human-AI Collaboration Design

Human-AI collaboration design is the skill of architecting systems where human judgment and AI capability combine to produce outcomes neither could achieve alone. It's not about using AI tools, it's about designing workflows, decision processes, and team structures that leverage the complementary strengths of human and artificial intelligence.

How It Emerges

This skillset emerges from upgraded thought patterns (Chapter 7) and behavioral defaults (Chapter 8). When you can think systemically about how decisions get made and have the behavioral flexibility to experiment with new approaches, you can design human-AI collaboration that actually works.

Leaders without upgraded thought patterns see AI as a tool to be used or a threat to be managed. Leaders with systemic thinking see AI as a component in a larger system that can be designed. The shift from "using AI" to "designing human-AI systems" requires the meta-cognitive capacity that comes from thought pattern upgrades.

Signs of Mastery

- You naturally think about decision processes, not just decisions

- You can articulate what AI should and shouldn't be trusted to do

- You've successfully designed human-AI workflows that outperform either alone

- You iterate on collaboration designs based on outcomes

Skillset Four: Strategic Sensemaking

Strategic sensemaking is the ability to synthesize disparate signals into coherent understanding and translate that understanding into strategic direction, especially when operating in ambiguity where no clear playbook exists. This isn't strategic planning, which assumes enough clarity to plan. It's the capacity to find clarity when none exists, to see patterns in noise, to know which signals matter when everything seems to matter.

How It Emerges

This skillset emerges from the integration of all seven components working together. Beliefs that allow for uncertainty. Mindsets oriented toward curiosity. Emotional capacity to tolerate ambiguity. Thought patterns that synthesize complexity. Behaviors that test hypotheses. Values that prioritize learning. Communication that creates shared understanding.

Strategic sensemaking requires the full orchestra. A leader with rigid beliefs can't make sense of information that contradicts those beliefs. A leader who can't tolerate emotional ambiguity will force premature clarity. A leader without systemic thought patterns will see isolated data points rather than patterns. Only when all components are upgraded and integrated does strategic sensemaking become available.

Signs of Mastery

- You find clarity in situations others experience as chaos
- You can articulate a strategic direction even with incomplete information
- Others seek you out when they can't make sense of what's happening

- Your strategic calls prove right more often than chance would predict

Skillset Five: Exponential Thinking

Exponential thinking is the capacity to anticipate and plan for non-linear change, recognizing that AI-driven transformation follows exponential rather than linear patterns, and adjusting strategy accordingly. Human brains evolved for linear prediction. If a threat moved toward us at a certain speed, we could estimate when it would arrive. But exponential change defeats linear intuition. What seems far away arrives suddenly. What seems manageable becomes overwhelming. Leaders without exponential thinking are perpetually surprised.

How It Emerges

This skillset emerges from upgraded mindsets (particularly the shift from risk avoidance to experimentation) combined with values that prioritize long-term positioning over short-term optimization. The mindset shift is essential. Risk-averse leaders discount exponential possibilities because they seem unlikely in any given moment. They optimize for the predictable near-term rather than the uncertain long-term. But leaders who have made the shift to experimentation can hold exponential scenarios as real possibilities worth preparing for, even when linear logic suggests otherwise.

Signs of Mastery

- You're rarely surprised by technological developments
- Your strategic planning accounts for non-linear scenarios
- You invest in capabilities before they're obviously necessary
- You can explain exponential dynamics to linear thinkers

The Emergence Pattern

These five skillsets don't develop through training programs, they emerge when your operating system components integrate. This is a crucial distinction. You can't attend a workshop on "Cognitive Flexibility" and expect to develop it if your underlying beliefs are rigid. You can't learn "Strategic Sensemaking" from a book if your emotional processing shuts down under ambiguity.

The emergence pattern works like this: as you upgrade individual components, they begin to work together in new ways. Upgraded beliefs enable upgraded mindsets. Upgraded emotional processing enables upgraded thought patterns. Eventually, the integration reaches a tipping point - and capabilities appear that weren't available before.

Jackie didn't develop these skillsets by trying to develop them directly. She developed them by doing the component work: examining her beliefs, upgrading her mindsets, building her emotional processing capacity. The skillsets emerged as a byproduct of that deeper work.

"I didn't stop being good at what got me here," she reflected. "I added what the new level required. The old skills didn't become irrelevant, they became insufficient. The emerging skillsets filled the gap."

This is why the architecture matters. The "7" (components) must come before the "5" (skillsets). The skillsets are the emergent property of an upgraded operating system - they can't be installed directly.

Integration in Action

To see how the five emerging skillsets work together, let's return to Sarah, the technology executive we met in Chapter 2.

When Sarah was promoted to lead her company's AI integration initiative, she brought the analytical rigor that had built her career. Every vendor proposal was scrutinized. Every pilot program was analyzed for potential failures. Within six months, the initiative had stalled, not because her analysis was wrong, but because her risk-prevention operating system was running in an environment that required risk tolerance.

Sarah's transformation illustrates the emergence pattern in practice.

Cognitive flexibility allowed her to hold multiple perspectives simultaneously. From her engineering team's view, AI threatened their craftsmanship. From the CEO's view, delay meant competitive disadvantage. Holding both revealed that the real problem wasn't the technology or the team. It was an implementation approach that assumed technical readiness could substitute for psychological readiness.

Emotional intelligence at scale helped her read the organizational mood: fear masquerading as technical skepticism. Rather than pushing harder, she created space for the fear to surface. Once the emotional reality was named, her team could engage with implementation rather than defending against it.

Human-AI collaboration design shaped her redesign of the implementation. The original plan positioned AI as replacing human judgment in code review. Her redesign positioned AI as augmenting human judgment, with engineers owning final calls on architecture decisions and AI learning from their corrections.

Strategic sensemaking helped her see beyond the immediate implementation. If this succeeded, it would become the model for AI adoption across the company. If it failed, it would set back AI adoption by years. This view changed her priorities from fast implementation to successful implementation.

Exponential thinking opened new strategic territory. What becomes possible if we're great at human-AI collaboration? The answer - reduced development cycles, unprecedented experimentation capacity, engineers elevated to creative work - shifted the project from "necessary modernization" to "competitive transformation."

No single skillset would have been sufficient. Together, the five capabilities enabled Sarah to transform a stalled implementation into a model for organizational AI adoption.

The skillsets didn't add. They multiplied.

Assessing Your Emerging Skillsets

Use this self-assessment to identify your highest-leverage development opportunities. For each skillset, rate yourself 1-5:

1. = Significant limitation
2. = Below where I need to be
3. = Adequate but not exceptional
4. = Clear strength
5. = Defining capability

Cognitive Flexibility

- I update my thinking quickly when new information contradicts my current view: ____

- I can argue positions I disagree with persuasively: ____

- I notice when my current approach isn't working and adapt: ____

- I hold multiple perspectives without needing premature resolution: ____

Emotional Intelligence at Scale

- I read the emotional state of a room within minutes: ____

- I notice organizational mood shifts before they become crises: ____

- I create psychological safety that enables risk-taking: ____

- I model emotional regulation that others learn from: ____

Human-AI Collaboration Design

- I know when to trust AI outputs and when to override them: ____

- I design AI implementations that maintain human capability: ____

- I understand both the potential and limitations of AI tools: ____

- I identify when human-AI collaboration is failing and why: ____

Strategic Sensemaking

- I anticipate second and third-order effects of decisions: ____

- I see patterns that others miss: ____

- I maintain a coherent mental model while updating with new information: ____

- I extract strategic insight from operational data: ____

Exponential Thinking

- I ask "what would 10x require?" rather than accepting incremental improvement: ____

- I see disruption possibilities before others do: ____
- I'm comfortable with the uncertainty of exponential change: ____
- I challenge linear assumptions, mine and others': ____

Interpreting Your Results

Your highest scores indicate where your operating system is already producing these capabilities. These are strengths to leverage.

Your lowest scores reveal your highest-leverage development opportunities. But remember: you don't develop these skillsets directly. You develop them by upgrading the underlying components.

If cognitive flexibility is low, return to the belief and mindset work in Chapters 4 and 5. If emotional intelligence at scale is limited, focus on emotional processing (Chapter 6) and communication (Chapter 10). If human-AI collaboration design needs development, revisit thought patterns (Chapter 7) and behavioral defaults (Chapter 8).

Scores of 3 deserve attention. Adequate isn't enough for AI-era leadership. A 3 might be your most important priority because it's easy to overlook what's merely adequate.

The assessment points you back to the component work. That's where development happens. The skillsets emerge from that foundation.

What Comes Next

You now understand the first two layers of the 7-5-3 Human Upgrade Code™: the seven components that form your internal architecture and the five skillsets that emerge when those components integrate.

But individual transformation, however profound, isn't enough.

Leadership happens in context - in teams, organizations, cultures. Part Four addresses the remaining two layers: the three foundations that scale your transformation through culture (House of Empathy™ in Chapter 12), and the five AI leadership shifts that position you to lead - not just survive - as AI transforms your industry (Chapter 13).

Let's continue to Part Four, where we explore how to deploy your upgraded operating system for maximum impact.

⁂

END OF PART THREE

PART FOUR

SYSTEMS, CULTURE AND THE FUTURE

From Personal Upgrade to Organizational Transformation

CHAPTER TWELVE

THE HOUSE OF EMPATHY™

BUILDING ORGANIZATIONAL CULTURE THAT SUSTAINS HIGH PERFORMANCE

Throughout Part Two, we explored the seven components of your leadership operating system. In Part Three, we saw the five premium skillsets that emerge when those components work together. You now have the architecture for personal transformation.

But personal transformation has limits. You can upgrade your own operating system, but you lead within systems. Within cultures. Within organizations that have their own patterns - patterns that either support or constrain individual change. Master every framework in this book personally, and you'll still hit a ceiling if your organization's culture punishes the very behaviors those frameworks require.

This is where AI-era leadership gets counterintuitive. As AI takes over more analytical, transactional, and routine work, what remains is distinctly human: connection, trust, meaning, belonging. The leaders and organizations that thrive won't be those with the most sophisticated AI implementations. They'll be those who build cultures where humans flourish *alongside* AI - where people feel safe enough to experiment, connected enough to collaborate, and valued enough to bring their full capability to work.

That requires empathy - not as a soft skill, but as organizational infrastructure.

The House of Empathy™ is the complete blueprint for building organizational culture that sustains high performance. It's built on three foundational blocks - Curiosity, Care and Courage - that create the cultural infrastructure enabling individual upgrades to scale through teams and organizations. These three foundations are the "3" in the 7-5-3 Human Upgrade Code™. Seven operating system components. Five premium skillsets. Three cultural foundations. Together, they form the timeless architecture for leadership transformation - personal and organizational. The Five AI Leadership Shifts™, which we'll explore in Chapter Thirteen, show you how to apply this architecture to the current moment.

In an era when AI can analyze, optimize and automate, the leaders who build Houses of Empathy will have the one competitive advantage that can't be replicated: cultures where people genuinely thrive.

This chapter shows you how to build one.

Jackie's Ceiling

We began this book with Jackie standing in a hospital corridor late one night, finally admitting she'd become the leader she swore never to be. She'd snapped at her Chief Medical Officer about transformation timelines, and the silence that followed told her everything.

Jackie did the personal work. Over the following months, she examined her beliefs about leadership and control. She shifted her mindset from certainty to curiosity. She developed emotional processing capacity that let her recognize when anxiety was driving reactive behavior. She caught her thought patterns before they ran her. She rebuilt her relationship with Dr. Martinez through a difficult conversation done well.

Her individual operating system was upgraded. But something was still broken.

"I've changed," she told me, frustration evident. "But the organization hasn't. My team still doesn't bring me problems until they're crises. People still won't experiment because they're afraid of failure. The culture I built over years of command-and-control leadership is still running - even though I'm not running it anymore."

Jackie had discovered what every leader eventually learns: personal transformation is necessary but not sufficient. To change how an organization operates, you have to change the culture that shapes how everyone operates.

She needed a framework for building culture as deliberately as she'd rebuilt herself.

The Architecture of Culture

A house without a foundation crumbles. A foundation without walls provides no shelter. Walls without a roof leave everyone exposed. Every structure requires all its elements, working together, to fulfill its purpose.

The same is true of organizational culture. Isolated initiatives - a psychological safety workshop here, a communication training there

- fail to create lasting change because they lack structural integrity. They are rooms without houses, walls without foundations.

The House of Empathy™ provides that structural integrity. It's a framework I've developed through years of organizational transformation work - a comprehensive architecture for building cultures where people thrive and organizations excel. Like any well-designed structure, it has a foundation that supports everything above it, pillars that bear the weight, and a roof that completes and protects the whole.

The framework extends your personal operating system upgrade to the organizational level. The internal work you've done on beliefs, mindsets, emotions, thoughts, behaviors, values, and communication creates your capacity for culture change. The House of Empathy™ shows you how to build cultures that develop that same capacity in others.

Why Culture Matters Now

Culture has always mattered, but AI makes it urgent. Organizations attempting AI transformation without adequate cultural foundation discover that their greatest obstacle isn't technology - it's people.

AI implementation requires psychological safety for experimentation. It requires learning velocity when skills become obsolete. It requires trust when roles change unexpectedly. It requires communication that handles uncertainty without generating panic. It requires conflict navigation when AI creates new tensions.

Organizations with strong cultures navigate AI transformation successfully. Organizations with weak cultures fragment under the pressure. The technology is available to everyone; the culture to implement it successfully is not.

Google's Project Aristotle, which studied what makes teams effective, found that psychological safety was the most important factor - more important than individual intelligence, resources, or structure. Teams where people felt safe to take interpersonal risks consistently outperformed teams where they didn't.

The House of Empathy™ builds that safety systematically, along with the other cultural elements high performance requires.

Jackie's culture had none of this. Her years of command-and-control leadership had created an organization optimized for execution, not experimentation. People knew how to follow orders brilliantly. They had no idea how to take initiative, challenge assumptions, or fail productively.

When she'd snapped at Dr. Martinez, she wasn't just revealing her own operating system - she was revealing the culture's. His response - looking down at his notes, avoiding her eyes - wasn't personal weakness. It was what the culture had trained him to do when a leader showed displeasure: go quiet, wait it out, don't make it worse.

That culture would never successfully transform. It couldn't tolerate the experimentation, the ambiguity, the productive failure that AI-era leadership requires.

Jackie needed to rebuild the house from the foundation up.

The Foundation: Curiosity, Care and Courage

Every structure needs a foundation strong enough to support everything built upon it. The House of Empathy™ rests on three foundational elements - the three Cs that make everything else possible.

Curiosity

Curiosity is the genuine desire to understand - to learn, to discover, to explore perspectives different from your own. It's the antidote to the certainty that creates blind spots and the judgment that shuts down learning.

Curious cultures ask questions rather than assume answers. They treat disagreement as data rather than disloyalty. They stay open to being wrong, which is the only way to become right about things that matter.

AI-era application: AI rewards curiosity exponentially. Leaders and organizations that stay curious about AI's capabilities, limitations, and applications learn faster than those who approach it with preconceptions. Curiosity enables the experimentation that AI adoption requires.

Jackie started with curiosity. Instead of telling her executive team what the AI implementation strategy should be, she asked: "What would you try if you knew you couldn't fail? What are we not seeing because we're too close to it?"

The first few meetings, people gave safe answers - the things they thought she wanted to hear. But she kept asking. Kept being genuinely curious. Kept responding to ideas with questions rather than judgments.

Dr. Martinez was the first to test whether the curiosity was real. "I think we're moving too fast on the diagnostic AI," he said - the same position that had triggered her snap months earlier. "Not because I'm resistant to change, but because I don't think the radiologists trust it yet. And if they don't trust it, they'll find ways to work around it."

Jackie felt the old impulse rise - the certainty that she was right, that resistance was the problem. But her upgraded operating system caught the pattern. "Tell me more about what you're seeing," she said. "What would help them trust it?"

Dr. Martinez's surprise was visible. This was not the response he'd expected. But it was the response the culture needed to see.

Care

Care is genuine concern for others' wellbeing - not as a strategy for getting results, but as a value in itself. Care creates the emotional foundation for trust, collaboration, and commitment.

Caring cultures notice when people struggle and respond with support rather than judgment. They invest in development because they genuinely want people to grow. They make decisions that consider human impact, not just financial outcomes.

AI-era application: AI transformation affects people's livelihoods, identities, and sense of worth. Organizations that demonstrate genuine care during this transition maintain trust and commitment. Organizations that treat people as resources to optimize lose both.

Care was harder for Jackie. Not because she didn't care - she cared deeply about patient outcomes, about organizational success - but because her version of care had become transactional. She cared about people performing well. She hadn't been caring about people as people.

The shift started small. She began asking her direct reports about their lives, not just their deliverables. When someone struggled, she asked how she could help instead of asking when the problem would be fixed. When the diagnostic AI pilot showed mixed results, she asked the team what they needed rather than stepping in to fix it herself.

"I realized," Jackie told me, "that I'd been caring about the mission so much that I forgot to care about the people executing it. And that was backwards. The mission only happens through the people. If I don't care about them, the mission suffers."

Courage

Courage is the willingness to act despite fear - to have difficult conversations, to challenge the status quo, to take risks in service of growth. Curiosity and care without courage produce nothing; courage converts insight into action.

Courageous cultures speak truth even when uncomfortable. They address problems early rather than letting them fester. They experiment even when success isn't guaranteed.

AI-era application: AI requires courage at every level. Courage to acknowledge that current approaches may be obsolete. Courage to invest in transformation before the need is urgent. Courage to make decisions about AI that affect people's work and worth.

Jackie's courage had never been in question - but it had been misdirected. She'd had the courage to push unpopular decisions, to demand results, to hold people accountable. What she hadn't had was the courage to be vulnerable - to admit uncertainty, to acknowledge mistakes, to let people see her struggle.

At the next all-hands meeting, Jackie did something unprecedented. She apologized.

"I've created a culture where people are afraid to fail," she said. "Where experimentation feels risky and disagreement feels dangerous. That's on me. I built that culture through years of behavior that valued execution over learning, certainty over curiosity, speed over wisdom."

She paused. Five hundred people waited.

"I'm working to change that. But I need your help. I need you to tell me when I'm slipping back into old patterns. I need you to bring me problems before they become crises. I need you to disagree with me when you think I'm wrong - because I'm wrong more often than I've let any of us admit."

The vulnerability was terrifying. It was also the most important thing she'd said in her three years as COO.

Your Foundation Assessment

Pause here. Assess your organization's foundation, the three Cs:

Curiosity: When was the last time someone in your organization said "I don't know" without fear? When disagreement surfaces, is it treated as data or disloyalty? Do people ask questions, or do they wait to be told?

Care: When someone struggles, does your organization respond with support or judgment? Is development genuine or transactional? Do decisions consider human impact beyond the spreadsheet?

Courage: Do people speak truth even when uncomfortable? Are problems addressed early or allowed to fester? Is vulnerability modeled or punished?

Be honest. The foundation you assess is the foundation you can build on, or must rebuild.

The Nine Pillars

With the foundation in place, we construct nine pillars, the operational elements that translate foundational values into organizational reality.

Pillar One: Build Trust

Trust is the main load-bearing pillar of the framework. Without trust, everything else becomes harder - communication is guarded, collaboration is superficial, change is resisted.

Leaders build trust through transparency, integrity, and consistency. Transparency means sharing information appropriately rather than hoarding it for power. Integrity means alignment between words and actions. Consistency means being predictable in your values and responses.

Trust takes time to build and moments to destroy. A single betrayal - saying one thing and doing another, sharing confidential information, throwing someone under the bus - can undo years of trust-building.

Jackie had destroyed trust through inconsistency. She'd said she valued innovation while punishing failure. She'd asked for feedback while responding defensively when she received it. She'd talked about empowerment while making all the decisions herself.

Rebuilding required consistency over time. Not one apology, but months of behavior that matched her new words. Every time she responded to a mistake with curiosity instead of blame, trust grew incrementally. Every time she asked for input and actually used it, people believed a little more.

"Trust is rebuilt in the small moments," Jackie observed. "Not the big speeches. The small moments where you could react the old way, and people are watching to see if you will."

Pillar Two: Understand One Another's World

Most organizational dysfunction stems from people not understanding each other's context. Engineering doesn't understand sales pressures; sales doesn't understand engineering constraints; neither understands what finance is dealing with. This lack of understanding breeds frustration, blame, and siloed thinking.

Understanding one another's world means investing time in learning what others actually do, what challenges they face, what they're trying to accomplish. It means asking questions rather than making assumptions. A simple practice: shadow someone in a different function for half a day. What you learn will change how you interpret their decisions.

Pillar Three: Express Appreciation and Recognition

Recognition is linked to higher job satisfaction, motivation, and loyalty - yet most people can count on one hand the times they've received genuine, specific appreciation from leaders. Generic praise doesn't land. Specific recognition transforms: "The way you handled that client escalation showed real composure under pressure." Recognition should be timely, specific and genuine.

Pillar Four: Prioritize Active Engagement

Active engagement means fostering a culture where employees participate, contribute and collaborate - where they have a voice in decisions that affect them. Research shows participative decision-making contributes to motivation, ownership and satisfaction. When people have input, they're more committed to outcomes, even when decisions don't go their way.

Pillar Five: Embrace Positive Perspective

Positive perspective involves cultivating optimism, resilience, and solutions-oriented mindset. This isn't toxic positivity that denies reality, it's genuine perspective that acknowledges difficulties while refusing to be paralyzed by them.

The leader's energy is contagious. If you consistently see problems, your team sees problems. If you consistently see possibilities, your team looks for them too.

Pillar Six: Navigate Conflict Constructively

This pillar extends the difficult conversation skills from individual capability to cultural norm. When conflict navigation is a shared capability, disagreements get addressed before they fester. Issues surface early while they're manageable.

Leaders who navigate conflict constructively facilitate collaboration, encourage healthy debate, and seek mutually beneficial solutions. They model that disagreement is not disloyalty.

Jackie brought me in to work with her leadership team on conflict navigation. We started where all transformation starts - with internal work. Each leader did individual coaching to examine their own patterns around conflict, the defaults that ran when conversations got difficult. Only then did we move to group facilitation sessions where the real culture shift happened. They practiced inviting diverse perspectives into every conversation - actively seeking out disagreement rather than avoiding it. They learned to treat pushback as data, to meet challenges with curiosity rather than defensiveness. They debriefed difficult conversations together and role-played scenarios where the goal wasn't winning but understanding.

"We turned conflict navigation into a team sport," Jackie said. "It stopped being something people dreaded and started being something we were genuinely good at."

Pillar Seven: Build Emotional Intelligence

Teams with high collective emotional intelligence read situations more accurately, respond more appropriately, and recover more quickly from setbacks. They notice when someone is struggling and respond with support. Building this pillar requires ongoing investment - in assessment, training, coaching and practice. Emotional intelligence isn't developed through a single workshop.

Pillar Eight: Promote Authentic Leadership

Authentic leadership means aligning actions with core values and exemplifying desired behaviors. Leaders are expected to show up as themselves, not as performances of what they think leaders should be.

Authentic leadership creates permission for others to be authentic too. When the CEO shares a genuine struggle, it signals that vulnerability is safe. When leaders perform leadership instead of embodying it, everyone else performs too, and performative cultures are brittle under pressure.

Pillar Nine: Foster Psychological Safety

Psychological safety isn't about being comfortable, it's about feeling safe enough to be uncomfortable. It's the confidence that you can raise a concern without being punished, challenge an idea without being ostracized, admit a mistake without being shamed.

Building psychological safety requires ongoing attention. It can be undermined by a single shaming incident, a dismissive response to a question, or a punishment for honest failure.

This was Jackie's ultimate goal, and her hardest challenge. She'd spent years making psychological safety impossible. Every snap, every dismissive response, every punishment for failure had taught people that speaking up was dangerous.

Rebuilding it required public failure tolerance. When the diagnostic AI pilot showed mixed results, Jackie gathered the team and asked what they'd learned, not what had gone wrong. When a junior analyst pushed back on a strategy she was championing, she thanked him publicly for the challenge.

"Every interaction is data," Jackie said. "People are constantly watching to see if it's really safe or if you're just saying it is. You have to prove it hundreds of times before they believe it."

Your Pillar Assessment

Consider your organization's nine pillars. Which is strongest? Which needs the most attention?

Most organizations have one or two pillars that are solid and several that are weak or missing entirely. The weak pillars constrain everything else - like a house with a missing wall, the structure doesn't hold.

What would change if you strengthened your weakest pillar? What becomes possible that isn't possible now?

That pillar is probably your highest-leverage culture investment. And unlike the foundation work that only leaders can do, pillar-building can engage your entire organization.

In AI transformation, psychological safety and trust tend to be the pillars under greatest strain - and the ones most essential to get right. If your assessment reveals weakness there, that's where to start.

The Roof: Shared Purpose and Growth

The roof completes the structure, integrating everything beneath and protecting the whole.

Supporting Personal and Professional Growth

People want to grow. When organizations support that growth - through learning opportunities, challenging assignments, coaching, and development - they tap into intrinsic motivation that no compensation package can match.

Supporting growth means understanding what each person is trying to become and helping them get there. It means managers are evaluated not just on output but on how much their people develop. It means creating paths forward that don't all lead through management - because not everyone wants to manage, but everyone wants to matter.

Creating Shared Purpose

At the pinnacle lies shared purpose - a living sense of why the work matters, felt by people throughout the organization. It's the answer to "Why do we do this?" that resonates not just intellectually but emotionally.

Shared purpose isn't a mission statement on a wall. It's the connection between daily work and something larger than individual achievement.

Jackie reconnected her organization to its purpose. Not through slogans or initiatives, but through the people they served. She brought patients into leadership meetings to share their experiences. She connected the transformation work to specific moments where better care could have prevented suffering.

"We'd gotten so focused on the process and the timeline that we forgot why we were doing this," she reflected. "When you're arguing about implementation details and a patient tells you about waiting three weeks for a diagnosis that could have taken three hours, the arguing stops. Purpose clarifies everything."

Building the House in the AI Era

The House of Empathy™ The isn't just good culture practice - it's the essential infrastructure for AI transformation.

Every element we've explored directly enables what AI demands: the foundation creates space for experimentation; trust allows honest conversation about fears and concerns; psychological safety enables the failure tolerance that learning requires; shared purpose keeps people connected to meaning when roles and workflows shift beneath them.

Without this infrastructure, AI transformation becomes a technical initiative imposed on a resistant culture. With it, AI transformation becomes a collective capability that the culture actively supports.

Jackie's organization didn't succeed with AI because they had better technology. They succeeded because they had a culture where people could experiment without fear, raise concerns without punishment, and adapt without losing their sense of purpose.

That's what the House of Empathy™ builds. Not a nice-to-have. The foundation for everything that comes next.

Jackie's House

Eighteen months after her corridor moment, Jackie's organization looked different.

The diagnostic system was live across three departments - not because Jackie had pushed it through, but because the teams had pulled it in. They'd experimented, failed productively, learned, and iterated. When problems arose, people brought them forward immediately rather than hiding them until they became crises.

Dr. Martinez had become one of the strongest advocates for the transformation - not because Jackie had convinced him, but because the culture now made it safe to experiment and the results spoke for themselves.

"I didn't just change how I lead," Jackie told me. "I changed what kind of organization this is. The House of Empathy gave me a framework for that change - something I could build deliberately rather than hoping the culture would shift because I had."

She paused. "The irony is that the culture change took longer than any of my previous initiatives. But it's also the only one that's going to last. Everything else I built was on a weak foundation. This one can hold weight."

From Culture to Capability

The House of Empathy™ creates the cultural infrastructure for transformation. But culture alone doesn't implement change - people do. And those people need specific guidance on how to lead through the unique challenges AI transformation presents.

The next chapter addresses what Jackie and every leader facing AI transformation needs to understand: the human work that makes technology work. You'll learn why AI amplifies both capability and dysfunction, how to navigate the emotional journey of AI adoption, and what distinguishes leaders who succeed at AI transformation from those who struggle.

The culture you build with the House of Empathy™ creates the conditions for success. Chapter Thirteen shows you how to lead within those conditions.

❧

CHAPTER THIRTEEN

THE FIVE AI LEADERSHIP SHIFTS™

The Mental Models That Determine Transformation Success

Two organizations. Same industry. Same size. Same technology budget. Same implementation partners.

A year later, one had transformed. AI was embedded in core operations, generating measurable impact, continuously improving through organizational learning. Employees talked about AI as enabling their work, making them more effective, freeing them for higher-value contributions.

The other had stalled. Pilots remained pilots. Adoption was spotty and reluctant. The technology sat largely unused while the organization continued operating as before. Employees talked about AI as threatening, disruptive, something management was forcing on them.

The difference wasn't technology. It was leadership.

The successful organization had leaders who understood that AI transformation is primarily a human challenge - that the technology is the easy part, and the leadership operating system upgrade is what determines success. The unsuccessful organization had leaders who thought buying the right technology was the job and were baffled when it didn't transform anything by itself.

The difference between these two organizations wasn't budget, tools, or even strategy. It was the mental models their leaders held about AI itself.

Throughout this book, you've done the deep work: upgrading the seven components of your internal operating system, developing the five premium skillsets, building the three cultural foundations of the House of Empathy™. Now, the Five AI Leadership Shifts™ show you how to deploy everything you've built in the context that matters most: leading through transformation.

In Chapter Five, you did the internal mindset work - the five psychological shifts that prepared your operating system for change. Here, we translate that internal preparation into external leadership practice. These five shifts represent fundamental changes in how you conceptualize and lead with AI. They're not about tools or technical skills - they're about the mental models that determine whether AI amplifies your leadership or undermines it.

The AI Leadership Paradox

Here's the paradox: AI amplifies human capability, which means it also amplifies human limitation. Organizations with strong leadership operating systems leverage AI to multiply their effectiveness.

Organizations with weak operating systems find AI multiplies their dysfunction.

AI doesn't fix broken cultures, but it will expose them. It doesn't resolve unclear strategy, but if strategy is unclear it will accelerate confusion. It doesn't compensate for poor leadership, it magnifies its impact.

This is why the operating system work we've explored throughout this book isn't separate from AI strategy - it's prerequisite to transformation success. Leaders who've upgraded their beliefs, mindsets, emotional processing, thought patterns, behaviors, values, and communication are equipped for what's ahead. Leaders who haven't will struggle regardless of their technical resources.

Shift One: From AI as Tool to AI as Collaborator

Most leaders approach AI the way they approach software: as a tool to be used, a system to be operated, a resource to be deployed. You give it inputs, it produces outputs. The relationship is transactional and hierarchical - you're the user, it's the used.

This mental model fundamentally limits what AI can do for you. Tools don't push back. Tools don't surface insights you didn't ask for. Tools don't get better at helping you as they learn your context and patterns.

The shift to AI as collaborator changes the relationship. You're not operating a system, you're working with a partner that has different capabilities than you do. You bring judgment, context, ethics and creativity. AI brings pattern recognition, information synthesis, tireless iteration and freedom from cognitive biases you can't escape.

Leaders who make this shift start asking different questions: "What would I want a collaborator to know about this problem?" instead of "What command do I enter?" They invest in the relationship - providing context, giving feedback, iterating on outputs. They treat AI's contributions as starting points for dialogue, not final answers to accept or reject.

The Shift in Practice

Alison, the marketing director whose belief architecture work we explored in Chapter 4, used to give AI simple commands: "Write an email about our new product." The results were generic, requiring extensive revision. She experienced AI as a mediocre tool that created more work than it saved.

When she shifted to treating AI as a collaborator, her approach changed entirely. She started by sharing context: "Here's what I know about our customers. Here's what makes this product different. Here's the tone that works for our brand. Here's what hasn't worked before." Then she engaged in dialogue: "What angles might I be missing? What would make this more compelling? How might different customer segments respond differently?"

The quality of outputs improved dramatically - not because the AI changed, but because the relationship changed. It was the same lesson Alison had learned about her own leadership: capability isn't fixed. It expands when you change how you engage with it.

The Mindset Upgrade Connection: This shift requires the upgrade from Control to Orchestration you developed in Chapter 5. Leaders who still need to control everything can't collaborate - with AI or with humans.

Shift Two: From AI as Threat to AI as Amplifier

The threat narrative dominates AI discourse: AI will take your job, make your skills obsolete, render human judgment unnecessary. This narrative triggers defensive responses - resistance, avoidance, minimization of AI's relevance to "real" leadership work.

The amplifier frame inverts this entirely. AI doesn't replace your capabilities - it multiplies them. Your judgment becomes more powerful when informed by AI analysis. Your communication becomes more effective when AI helps you understand your audience. Your strategic thinking becomes sharper when AI surfaces patterns you couldn't see.

The key insight: AI amplifies whatever operating system it's connected to. Leaders with upgraded operating systems - clear thinking, emotional regulation, strong values, effective communication - find AI amplifies their effectiveness. Leaders with dysfunctional operating systems find AI amplifies their dysfunction.

This is why the work you've done in this book matters so much. The operating system upgrade isn't separate from AI readiness - **it is AI readiness.** You've been preparing for this amplification throughout every chapter.

The Shift in Practice

David initially saw AI as a threat to the expertise that had defined his career. "If AI can do the analysis, what do we contribute?" His team sensed his ambivalence and mirrored it - they minimized AI's capabilities, found reasons it couldn't work for their specific needs, and continued doing things the old way.

When he shifted to the amplifier frame, everything changed. He realized AI could handle routine analysis, freeing his team to focus on judgment calls, stakeholder relationships and strategic interpretation - the work that actually required human expertise. AI didn't threaten his team's value; it amplified it by removing the routine work that had been burying their real contributions.

His team's output quality increased. Their strategic impact increased. Their job satisfaction increased. AI became an enabler, not a threat.

The Mindset Upgrade Connection: This shift draws on multiple upgrades from Chapter Five. The move from Certainty to Curiosity transforms threat responses into exploration - asking "What might AI amplify in my leadership?" The move from Expertise to Learning Velocity, which David experienced directly, reframes AI from competitor to accelerant.

Shift Three: From AI Expertise to AI Fluency

Many leaders believe they need to become AI experts to lead effectively in the AI era. They feel pressure to understand machine learning algorithms, neural network architectures, and technical implementation details. This belief creates paralysis, the expertise bar feels impossibly high.

The shift to fluency reframes the requirement entirely. You don't need to be an AI expert any more than you need to be a financial expert to lead a company with a CFO. You only need fluency - enough understanding to have intelligent conversations, ask good questions, evaluate recommendations, and make informed decisions.

AI fluency means understanding what AI can and can't do, recognizing when AI might help with a challenge, knowing what questions to ask technical teams, and being able to evaluate AI-related proposals and results. It's conversational competence, not technical mastery.

The Shift in Practice

Early in her transformation journey, before the operating system work we explored in Chapter 12, Jackie felt paralyzed by AI decisions because she "wasn't technical enough." She deferred to IT on all AI-related matters, which meant strategic decisions were being made by people optimizing for technical elegance rather than patient impact.

When she shifted to fluency, she stopped trying to understand how AI worked technically and started asking different questions: "What problem does this solve? How will we know if it's working? What could go wrong? What do patients and staff experience? How does this fit our strategy?"

These were questions she was perfectly qualified to ask - and her leadership became essential rather than peripheral to AI decisions. She didn't need to know how the technology worked. She needed to know what it was for.

The Mindset Upgrade Connection: This shift requires the upgrade from Expertise to Learning Velocity - the capacity to learn faster than your environment changes. Leaders anchored in their existing expertise feel threatened by domains they haven't mastered. Leaders oriented toward learning velocity embrace the opportunity to develop new fluencies. They know that in the AI era, what you can learn matters more than what you already know.

Shift Four: From AI Implementation to AI Integration

Implementation is project thinking: define scope, allocate resources, execute plan, declare completion. This approach treats AI as something to install - a bounded initiative with a beginning, middle, and end.

Integration is transformation thinking: weave AI into how the organization thinks, decides, and operates. There's no end date because integration is ongoing - a continuous evolution of human-AI collaboration across every function and process.

Organizations stuck in implementation mode run pilot after pilot without scaling. They treat AI as a series of projects rather than a fundamental shift in how work happens. They wait for "the AI project" to finish before returning to business as usual - not understanding that business as usual has permanently changed.

Leaders who make this shift stop asking "When will AI be implemented?" and start asking "How is AI changing how we operate?" They focus on building organizational capacity for continuous evolution, not completing discrete initiatives.

The Shift in Practice

A retail company launched an "AI transformation initiative" with a one-year timeline, dedicated budget and project team. The project hit its milestones and was declared a success. But actual AI adoption across the organization was minimal, the project had built capabilities that sat unused because they weren't integrated into how people actually worked.

A competitor took a different approach: no big initiative, just continuous integration. They started small - AI assisting with a single customer service function - then expanded based on learning. They integrated AI into existing workflows rather than building separate AI workflows. They measured adoption and impact, not project milestones.

Two years later, the competitor had AI deeply embedded in operations while the "successful" initiative remained largely unused.

The Mindset Upgrade Connection: This shift requires the upgrade from Risk Avoidance to Experimentation. Implementation seeks certainty before acting. Integration embraces ongoing experimentation as the only path forward.

Shift Five: From AI Efficiency to AI Capability

The dominant AI narrative focuses on efficiency: AI will make you faster, cheaper, more productive. Do the same things with fewer resources. Automate routine work. Cut costs.

Efficiency is real, but it's the least interesting thing AI offers. The transformational opportunity is capability - using AI to do things that were previously impossible, not just doing existing things faster.

What becomes possible when you can analyze every customer interaction in real-time? When you can personalize at scale? When you can simulate hundreds of strategic scenarios before committing? When you can synthesize information across domains that no human could hold in mind simultaneously?

Leaders stuck on efficiency ask: "How can AI help us do this faster?" Leaders oriented toward capability ask: "What becomes possible that wasn't possible before?" The first question leads to incremental improvement. The second leads to transformation.

The Shift in Practice

A manufacturing company initially used AI to optimize their existing processes - shaving costs, reducing waste, improving throughput. Valuable, but incremental.

Then a leader asked a different question: "What could we offer customers that we couldn't before?" The team took an innovative look at what customers actually cared about - and discovered needs the company had always considered unfeasible to address. With AI, they could now detect issues before customers knew they existed, predict needs before customers articulated them, and customize solutions that would have been economically impossible at scale.

They went from selling products to selling outcomes - a transformation that efficiency thinking never would have revealed.

The Mindset Upgrade Connection: This shift requires the upgrade from Individual Decisions to Collaborative Intelligence. Efficiency thinking is about optimizing individual performance. Capability thinking is about what becomes possible when human and artificial intelligence work together.

The Complete 7-5-3 Human Upgrade Code™ Architecture

You've now experienced the full 7-5-3 Human Upgrade Code™:

- **Seven Components** formed your internal operating system foundation

- **Five Skillsets** emerged when those components integrated

- **Three Foundations** enabled your transformation to scale through culture

This architecture isn't just a framework for reading a book. It's a diagnostic and development methodology you can return to throughout your career. Most leadership challenges can be located somewhere on this map. Every growth opportunity can be traced to one of these layers.

The Five AI Leadership Shifts™ are how you apply this timeless architecture to the current moment. The specific shifts - from Tool to

Collaborator, from Threat to Amplifier, from Expertise to Fluency, from Implementation to Integration, from Efficiency to Capability - reflect where most leaders are stuck today. Future shifts will emerge as AI capabilities expand and new mental model traps become apparent. But the underlying 7-5-3 architecture will remain your foundation.

The principle is constant: your internal operating system determines your external effectiveness. Leaders who've done the upgrade work will leverage AI to multiply their impact. Leaders who haven't will find AI multiplies their dysfunction.

You've done the work. Now lead the transformation.

THE ONGOING JOURNEY

FROM TRANSFORMATION TO WAY OF LIFE

We began this book with a screensaver.

Jackie, the healthcare COO, watched those shifting patterns and saw her own mind - beautiful but restless, moving constantly but getting nowhere, running sophisticated programs that produced impressive activity but not the results she most needed.

Her operating system had reached its limits. The patterns that had brought her success were now creating her struggles. Something had to change.

By now, you probably recognize something similar in yourself. Not the specific details, your story is your own, but the dynamic. The sense that the way you've been operating, however successful, isn't adequate for what lies ahead. The intuition that some kind of upgrade is needed.

This final chapter addresses what comes after the insight, how to sustain the transformation you've begun and make continuous development a way of life rather than a project with an end date.

The Sustainability Challenge

Change initiated is not change sustained. The patterns you've been running for years or decades don't disappear because you've gained awareness of them. They remain available, ready to reassert themselves the moment conditions favor them.

Stress activates old patterns. When cognitive load increases, the brain reaches for whatever response requires least effort, and your old defaults are well-practiced. A difficult quarter, a challenging relationship, a health issue, a family crisis - any of these can trigger reversion to patterns you thought you'd left behind.

Environments reinforce patterns. The relationships, structures, and expectations around you were built when your old operating system was running. They may actively pull you back toward familiar ways of being, even unconsciously.

Time erodes attention. The focused awareness you brought to your development naturally fades as other priorities claim your attention. Without sustained attention, old patterns gradually return.

Sustainability isn't automatic. It requires deliberate design - practices, relationships, and environments that support your continued development.

The Five Questions

Of all the sustainability practices available, one stands out for its combination of simplicity, power, and adaptability: a weekly reflection practice structured around key questions.

I give all my clients these questions to work through each week. Fifteen minutes creates a rhythm of reflection that prevents drift, catches regression early, and maintains connection to your development.

Question One: What am I fighting that I need to accept? Notice where you're expending energy resisting reality rather than responding to it. Strategic acceptance - starting with what is rather than what you wish - frees resources for effective action.

Question Two: Did I live my values this week? Be honest: was there alignment between what you say is important and how you actually showed up? This question keeps values operational rather than aspirational.

Question Three: What unhelpful stories is my mind telling? Identify the thoughts creating stress without enabling action - the thought patterns running unchecked. Naming them creates distance that enables different responses.

Question Four: Where is my attention going? Notice what's actually receiving your focus versus what deserves it. Present-moment leadership requires attention control.

Question Five: What's one thing I'm committed to doing next week, even if I don't feel like it? Pick something that matters and commit regardless of whether you feel confident, ready, or motivated.

This is committed action despite discomfort - strategic discomfort in weekly practice.

Sustaining Your Upgrade

Understanding the five questions is the beginning. Sustaining your operating system upgrade requires understanding why change is so difficult, and designing systems that work with your psychology, not against it.

Why Insight Isn't Enough

Research consistently shows that information and awareness account for only a small percentage of actual behavior change. Leaders leave workshops inspired and committed, then return to their organizations and continue doing exactly what they did before. Not because they're resistant or lacking willpower, but because the forces maintaining their current patterns are stronger than the forces for change.

Four forces work against you:

Defaults are efficient. Your current patterns require no cognitive effort, they run automatically. New patterns require conscious attention, which is scarce under pressure.

Systems reinforce patterns. Your environment - relationships, expectations, structures - was built around your current operating system. It actively pulls you back to familiar ways of being.

Identity resists change. Your operating system has become part of who you are. Changing it can feel like losing yourself, even when the change is positive.

Short-term costs precede long-term benefits. New behaviors feel awkward and produce worse results initially. The payoff comes later, if you persist.

The Discomfort Ratio

Through my work teaching leadership at MIT Professional education, I've developed what I call the discomfort ratio - the percentage of development time that involves genuine challenge versus comfortable repetition of what you already know.

The sweet spot for sustainable growth falls between twenty-five and thirty-five percent productive discomfort. Below fifteen percent, you're coasting - staying busy without developing. Above forty percent, you risk overwhelm and burnout.

Most leaders dramatically underestimate how much time they spend in the comfort zone. They feel busy and stressed, which they interpret as evidence of growth. But busyness and stress aren't the same as developmental discomfort. The question isn't whether you're working hard, it's whether you're working on the edges of your current capability.

The Stakeholder Advantage

Marshall Goldsmith's Stakeholder Centered Coaching methodology, which informs my practice, demonstrates the power of involving others in behavior change. The approach involves selecting stakeholders who observe your behavior regularly, informing them of what you're working on, asking for monthly feedforward - suggestions for the future rather than feedback on the past - and following up consistently to demonstrate commitment.

This methodology works because accountability increases follow-through, external perception provides a reality check, and relationships strengthen through the process. You may think you're changing, but stakeholders tell you whether they're experiencing that change.

As a certified Stakeholder Centered Coach who has guided numerous clients through this process, here's what I've learned: behavioral change is necessary but not sufficient. You can genuinely transform how you operate, but if the people around you still perceive you through the lens of your old patterns, the change doesn't fully land. Stakeholder Centered Coaching bridges that gap - it moves you from internal transformation to external perception change.

Most of my clients start with the operating system work in this book, then continue working with me through Stakeholder Centered Coaching to ensure their behavioral changes are seen and experienced by the people who matter most. If you're serious about making your transformation stick, this is how you close the gap between who you've become and how others experience you.

The Integration Timeline

How long does an operating system upgrade take? Longer than you hope, shorter than you fear.

Simple behavioral adjustments can show progress in weeks. Deeper pattern changes typically require three to six months of consistent practice. Foundational belief system upgrades may take a year or more.

The timeline depends on how entrenched the current patterns are, how much environmental support or resistance exists, and how consistently you practice new behaviors. But change is possible. Every leader I've worked with who committed to the process has upgraded their operating system. Not perfectly, the old patterns don't disappear entirely, but enough to show up differently, to produce different results, to become the leader their current challenges require.

The question isn't whether you can change. You can. The question is whether you'll do the work consistently enough, long enough, for change to take root.

The Multiplier Effect

The operating system you build doesn't just affect your own leadership, it shapes everyone your leadership touches. Your patterns become the patterns your team learns. Your culture becomes the culture others absorb. Your way of operating becomes the model for those who follow you.

This is both responsibility and opportunity. The work you do on yourself ripples outward in ways you may never fully see. The leader who develops emotional intelligence creates conditions where others develop it too. The leader who models curiosity creates permission for questions. The leader who navigates conflict constructively teaches others that conflict can be generative.

When you sustain your operating system upgrade, you're building more than personal effectiveness. You're building capacity - in yourself, in your team, in your organization - for the kind of leadership this moment demands.

Development as Identity

The deepest form of sustainability comes when continuous development becomes part of your identity, not something you do but Who You Are.

Leaders who sustain transformation over the long term don't think of development as a phase they went through. They think of themselves as people who are always developing, always learning, always working on their operating systems. Growth isn't an activity they engage in; it's a dimension of how they exist in the world.

This identity shift transforms the experience of development. Instead of feeling like extra work, it becomes integral to how you lead. Instead of requiring motivation, it becomes as natural as breathing, something you do because it's who you are.

Your Continuing Invitation

The frameworks in this book - the 7-5-3 Human Upgrade Code™ - are tools for a journey, not destinations to reach. Use them, adapt them, return to them as your development unfolds.

Remember the principle that underlies everything: strategic discomfort. The growth you most need will require the discomfort you most want to avoid. The upgrade that would transform your leadership is probably the one that feels hardest to install.

You don't have to wait for a crisis to do this work. You can choose the discomfort of growth deliberately, making transformation a way of life rather than a response to emergency.

A FINAL REFLECTION

I began my own operating system work not by choice but by necessity - a health crisis in 2013 that cracked open patterns I had spent decades reinforcing. Through that painful, beautiful process of rewiring, I discovered something I wish I had known earlier: you don't have to wait for a crisis. You can choose strategic discomfort deliberately.

The leaders I've watched transform - truly transform, not just adjust at the margins - share something in common. They made a decision that their development mattered. Not because it was comfortable, not because it was easy, but because becoming a better leader was integral to who they wanted to be.

They did the work on beliefs when it would have been easier to keep the old ones. They upgraded mindsets when the familiar orientation felt safer. They developed emotional intelligence when suppression seemed more efficient. They rewired thought patterns when the old ones were automatic. They modified behavioral defaults when the habits were ingrained. They clarified values when ambiguity was more convenient. They upgraded communication when the old approach was well-practiced.

And they sustained these upgrades - not through heroic willpower but through intelligent design of the practices, relationships, and environments that supported their continued growth.

You can do the same. The operating system you're running right now, whatever its limitations, brought you to this point. It has served you. But if you're reading this final chapter, you probably sense that it's time for an upgrade - that the leader you need to become requires capabilities your current system can't support.

That upgrade is possible. We've mapped the territory together. The complete 7-5-3 Human Upgrade Code™ architecture is now yours.

The only question remaining is the one we started with: Are you ready to begin?

Not to complete the journey - that's not how this works. But to begin, and to keep beginning, for as long as your leadership matters.

Which is to say: for the rest of your life.

The future belongs to leaders who can make this upgrade. I believe you're one of them.

Now go build the operating system your leadership deserves.

❧

END OF PART FOUR

ACKNOWLEDGMENTS

Three forces shaped this book.

My grandmother planted the first seed. She created the only space free from the pressure to conform - where I could be fully myself. *"You're not broken - you're different. And different is exactly what the world needs."* She never got to read these pages. But what she gave me is what I now give every client: a safe space to see clearly, and permission to grow into who they're meant to become. This book exists because she showed me that transformation begins in small, safe spaces.

My husband saw what this could become before I did. He believed in Leaderwired when it was just fragments scribbled between client sessions - and believed in me when I didn't. He pushed me to think ten times bigger when settling for safe would have been easy. The best ideas in this book came from our conversations, including the screensaver metaphor that unlocked everything. The courage to put it into the world came from watching him never waver. He is my home.

My clients taught me everything I know about transformation. They brought me their challenges and trusted me enough to go where the real work lived. They let me witness the moment an outdated operating system revealed itself as the ceiling - and the breakthrough that followed. Every methodology here was shaped in our work together. They showed me that transformation runs both ways: in helping them upgrade, I was continuously evolving too.

To you, holding this book: you are here because you sense what got you here won't get you there. The world doesn't need leaders running harder on outdated systems. It needs leaders willing to upgrade.

You've done more than read - you've begun the rewiring.

WHERE THE WORK LIVES

If this book did its job, you're not the same reader who opened Chapter One.

Something has shifted. Maybe you've named a belief you didn't know you held. Maybe you've traced a pattern back to its origin and felt the grip loosen. Maybe you're sitting with the uncomfortable recognition that your greatest strength has a shadow - and you're ready to work with it.

That shift is the beginning. But as Chapter Fourteen made clear, the forces that maintain current patterns are strong. Defaults are efficient. Environments reinforce old code. Identity resists rewiring. The leaders who sustain transformation are the ones who design support systems around the change they've committed to making.

Here's where that support lives.

Diagnose
The Leaderwired™ Assessment

The diagnostic work in this book gave you a starting point. The Leaderwired™ Assessment gives you precision.

This comprehensive evaluation maps where you stand across all three dimensions of the 7-5-3 Human Upgrade Code™ - your seven operating system components, five emerging skillsets, and three cultural foundations. It makes visible what self-reflection alone cannot: the hidden architecture of your internal operating system, including the patterns most deeply encoded and therefore most invisible to you.

UNLOCK YOUR ASSESSMENT

STEP 1: Visit leaderwired.com/assessment

STEP 2: Enter your unique access code:

ALC-7K4M-9P3X-R2W8

STEP 3: Enter your email and begin your assessment

Your personalized report will reveal your strengths and development priorities across all critical dimensions of AI-ready leadership.

This assessment is exclusively for Leaderwired readers. Please keep your access code confidential.

Connect
The Leaderwired ™ Collective

Operating system upgrades don't happen in isolation. The leaders who transform sustainably are the ones who surround themselves with others doing the same work.

The Leaderwired ™ Collective is a community for leaders committed to ongoing development - a space for shared learning, honest conversation, and the kind of accountability that makes transformation stick. Because the multiplier effect works both ways: your growth accelerates when you're around people who are growing too.

www.Leaderwired.com/collective

Transform
Executive Coaching

Jackie, Marcus, David, Sarah, Alison - every leader in this book did their deepest work in partnership with a coach. Not because they couldn't see their patterns alone, but because operating systems are designed to protect themselves from examination. The patterns most in need of upgrading are the ones most invisible from the inside.

As an ICF Master Certified Coach - a credential held by fewer than 1% of coaches globally - and a Marshall Goldsmith Certified Stakeholder Centered Coach, I bring the same methodology you've experienced in these pages to one-on-one and team engagements. The operating system work creates the internal shift. Stakeholder Centered Coaching ensures that shift is seen and experienced by the people who matter most.

If you're ready to close the gap between the leader you are and the leader this moment requires, let's talk.

www.Leaderwired.com/coaching

Scale
Keynotes, Workshops and Team Development

Individual transformation is necessary but not sufficient. If Chapter Twelve taught you anything, it's that culture either enables or constrains every upgrade you make. The House of Empathy™ isn't built by one leader alone - it's built by leadership teams who commit to the work together.

I bring the Leaderwired methodology to organizations through keynote presentations, leadership workshops, and team development engagements - designed to move entire leadership cultures from out-dated operating systems to the architecture this era demands.

www.Leaderwired.com/speaking

The upgrade doesn't end with the last page. It begins there.

Web: www.Leaderwired.com   www.AnnaBarnhill.com

Email: info@annabarnhill.com

LinkedIn: www.linkedin.com/in/annabarnhillmcc

ABOUT THE AUTHOR

Anna Barnhill has spent sixteen years studying why accomplished leaders get stuck - and how they break through. Her work integrates psychology, behavioral science and AI-era leadership.

Anna is an IOC Professional Fellow at McLean Hospital/Harvard Medical School and teaches leadership at MIT Professional Education. She is an ICF Master Certified Coach - a credential held by fewer than 1% of coaches worldwide - and a Marshall Goldsmith Certified Coach. Her writing on leadership appears in *Forbes*.

She has coached executives at Fortune 500 companies, closing the gap between what they know and the impact they make.

Anna's methodology emerged from both research and lived experience. In 2013, a year of health crises forced her to dismantle the operating system that had driven her success - and discover it was the same system holding her back. *Leaderwired* is what she rebuilt, pressure-tested through thousands of coaching hours.

Anna lives in Medford, Oregon, with her husband, Justin. She believes different is exactly what the world needs - and she's still proving her grandmother right.